DOMINOES

Little House on the Prairie

LEVEL THREE   **1000 HEADWORDS**

OXFORD
UNIVERSITY PRESS

Great Clarendon Street, Oxford OX2 6DP

Oxford University Press is a department of the University of Oxford.
It furthers the University's objective of excellence in research, scholarship,
and education by publishing worldwide in

Oxford New York

Auckland Cape Town Dar es Salaam Hong Kong Karachi
Kuala Lumpur Madrid Melbourne Mexico City Nairobi
New Delhi Shanghai Taipei Toronto

With offices in

Argentina Austria Brazil Chile Czech Republic France Greece
Guatemala Hungary Italy Japan Poland Portugal Singapore
South Korea Switzerland Thailand Turkey Ukraine Vietnam

OXFORD and OXFORD ENGLISH are registered trade marks of
Oxford University Press in the UK and in certain other countries

This edition © Oxford University Press 2010

The moral rights of the author have been asserted

Database right Oxford University Press (maker)

First published in Dominoes 2004

2016 2015

10 9

ISBN: 978 0 19 424817 4 BOOK
ISBN: 978 0 19 424775 7 BOOK AND MULTIROM PACK
MULTIROM NOT AVAILABLE SEPARATELY

No unauthorized photocopying

Printed in China

This book is printed on paper from certified and well-managed sources.

ACKNOWLEDGEMENTS

Illustrations by: Alan Marks

The publisher would like to thank the following for permission to reproduce photographs: Alamy
Images pp12 (farm buildings on the prarie/Robert Francis), 73 (Eminem/Roy Tee/S.I.N);
Corbis pp iv (Indian & son), iv (grey wolves/mary Ann McDonald), iv (classroom of Montana
schoolhouse/Joseph Sohm:Chromo Sohm Inc.), iv (tornado in a cornfield/Aaron Horowitz,
19 (grey wolf/Tom Brakefield), 33 (Chief Joseph by Edward S. Curtis/Christie's Images), 70
(Indian blanket/Christie's Images), 71 (abandoned cabin/George D. Lepp); Getty Images
pp iv (prarie fire/Terry Donnelly/Stone), 73 (family barbecue/Ty Allison/Taxi), 73 (sailing
boat/Antony Edwards/The Image Bank); Masterfile pp55 (bald eagle/Dale Sanders), 72
(young boy/Kevin Dodge), 72 (boy with baseball glove/David Schmidt); OUP pp iv (gold
coins/Photodisc), 6 (trees at sunset/Digital Vision), 13 (reflection on water/Photodisc), 60
(fire/Photodisc), 72 (teen girl smilingPhotodisc), 73 (trophy/Photodisc), 73 (dolphins/Corel);
SuperStock p25 (Navajo Monument Valley Arizona, USA/Ray Manley).

Cover: Corbis (Covered wagon/Jan Butchofsky-Houser)

DOMINOES

Series Editors: Bill Bowler and Sue Parminter

Little House on the Prairie

Laura Ingalls Wilder

Text adaptation by Jann Huizenga

Illustrated by Alan Marks

Laura Ingalls Wilder was born in Wisconsin in 1867. When she was a child she moved with her family to Kansas – the part of her life she describes in *Little House on the Prairie*. From Kansas the family moved on to Minnesota and then South Dakota. Laura started writing about her life when she was sixty-five years old, and wrote a number of popular and successful books describing her childhood and marriage. She died in 1957.

OXFORD
UNIVERSITY PRESS

BEFORE READING

The story *Little House on the Prairie* happens in America in the 1870s. The house is in the middle of wild country.

Which things do you think will be important in the story? Tick the boxes.

a ☐ Indians

b ☐ gold

c ☐ wolves

d ☐ school

e ☐ a fire

f ☐ strong winds

Chapter 1

The Ingalls family goes West

A long time ago, **Pa** and **Ma** and Mary and Laura and Baby Carrie left their little house in Wisconsin. They drove away and left it lonely and empty among the big trees, and they never saw that little house again. They were going to Indian country.

Pa said there were too many people in Wisconsin now. Wild animals did not stay in a country where there were so many people, so Pa didn't want to stay. He liked a country where the animals lived without fear. He liked to see them looking at him in the forest and eating fruit from the trees.

In the long winter evenings Pa talked to Ma about the Western country. 'Let's go see the West,' he said. 'The land is flat and the grass grows thick and high. Animals run freely and there are no **settlers**. Only **Indians** live there.'

'Oh, Charles, must we go now?' Ma said. 'The weather's so cold and our warm house is so comfortable.'

'If we are going this year, we must go now,' said Pa. 'We can't cross the Mississippi River after the ice breaks.'

So Pa sold the little house in Wisconsin. With Ma's help, he made a **canvas** cover for their **wagon**. They put everything into the wagon except their beds and tables and chairs. Pa could make new ones out West.

The next morning when it was still dark, Ma gently shook Mary and Laura until they got up. By the light of the fire she helped them dress warmly. They put on warm dresses and heavy coats. Grandmother, Grandfather, aunts, and uncles were all there to say good-bye to them.

Pa put his gun inside the wagon where he could reach it quickly. He put his **fiddle** between two blankets in order to

Pa father

Ma mother

settler someone who goes to live in wild land

Indian people who lived in North America before white people

canvas thick cloth

wagon a big open car pulled by horses

fiddle you can play music on this; a violin

1

keep it safe. Their dog Jack went under the wagon, and they drove away.

'When we get to the West,' Pa said to Laura, 'you'll see a papoose.'

'What's a papoose?' she asked.

'A papoose is a little brown Indian baby,' Pa explained.

It was a long, long way to Indian country. Almost every day the horses travelled as far as they could; almost every night Pa and Ma stopped in a new place. They rode across the wide Mississippi River before the ice broke, and crossed many other rivers and **creeks**.

One day Pa sold the tired brown horses and got two small young black horses with soft gentle eyes and long tails. 'They're western horses,' Pa said. 'Very strong but very gentle.' When Laura asked what their names were, Pa said that she and Mary could choose names for the horses. So they called one 'Pet' and the other 'Patty'.

They had travelled across Wisconsin, Minnesota, Iowa, and Missouri. All that long way, their little dog Jack had walked along under the wagon. Pa sat up front, holding the **reins**. Ma sat next to him, straight and quiet. Baby Carrie slept in soft blankets in the back. Now they were crossing Kansas, an endless flat land covered with tall grass. Day after day they saw nothing but grass and a big sky. There was nothing new to do and nothing new to look at.

'Ma, can't we get out and run behind the wagon?' Laura said. 'My legs are so tired.'

'No, Laura,' Ma said.

'I'm hungry. I want to **camp** now!'

Then Ma said, 'Laura.' That was all she said, but Laura understood that she should stay quiet.

'We're coming to a creek or river,' Pa said. 'Girls, can you see those trees? That's where we'll camp tonight.'

Suddenly the road went down and they arrived at the creek.

creek a narrow valley with straight sides and a river at the bottom

reins strings that are tied to a horse's head and that you pull to make it go one way or the other

camp to stop on a long journey in order to eat and sleep somewhere in the open country

Pet and Patty stopped to drink. The sound of fast-running water filled the still air. The river was silver and blue and the water ran quickly in the middle.

'The creek's really high,' Pa said. 'But I guess we can cross it.' Pa looked at Ma. 'What do you say, Caroline?'

'Yes, Charles,' Ma answered. 'I think we can.'

So the wagon went forward. Soon the wheels were in deep water. 'The horses may have to swim out there in the middle,' Pa said. 'But we'll get across all right, Caroline.'

Laura thought of Jack and said, 'I wish Jack could ride in the wagon, Pa.'

Pa did not answer. He was busy with the horses, pulling their reins. Ma said, 'Jack can swim, Laura. He'll be fine.'

Then suddenly the wagon lifted and rocked, and Laura knew they were in the creek. Mary hid under the blankets. She was afraid of the water. But Laura was excited.

Ma said loudly, 'Lie down, girls! Don't move!'

Mary and Laura dropped flat on the bed. When Ma spoke like that, they obeyed her. Ma's arm pulled a blanket over them, heads and all. Laura felt the wagon turning. The water made so much noise. Then Pa's voice frightened Laura. 'Take the horses, Caroline!' he said.

Suddenly Pa was gone. Ma sat alone, holding the reins with both hands. Mary hid her face in the blankets again, but Laura sat up and looked out. She couldn't see anything but water everywhere and three heads in the water – Pet's head, Patty's head, and Pa's small wet head. Pa's hand was holding Pet's head and he was talking calmly to the horses. Ma's face was white and frightened. Mary was crying and Laura felt cold and sick. She closed her eyes, but she could still see the terrible water with Pa in it. For a long time the wagon rocked in the water.

Finally the front wheels hit the ground and Pa shouted. Laura saw the wet horses climbing out of the water. Pa was running beside them, shouting 'Get up! Get up! Good girls!' And then the horses and the wagon stood still, safely out of that creek.

Pa was wet and tired. 'Oh, Charles!' Ma cried.

'Calm down, Caroline,' said Pa. 'We're all safe. All's well that ends well.' But Laura was still frightened. She knew they were lucky to be alive. Suddenly she shouted, 'Oh, where's Jack?'

They had forgotten Jack and could not see him anywhere. Pa walked up and down the creek looking everywhere for him. But Jack was gone. There was nothing to do but go on.

Laura tried not to cry. She looked back all the way, but she saw nothing except hills and trees.

Soon Pa stopped the horses. He was ready to camp. Mary and Laura climbed to the ground, too. Pa seemed sad. He did not sing while he worked as he usually did. 'I don't know what we'll do in a wild country without a good dog,' he said.

Pa made a fire and brought water from the creek. Mary and Laura helped Ma make a supper of salted **pork**, **cornbread**, and coffee. As they ate, purple shadows closed around the campfire. The wide **prairie** was dark and still.

Then Laura heard a long, frightening cry from the dark prairie.

'Wolves,' Pa said. 'I wish Jack was still with us.'

Laura felt like crying, but she knew she must be strong. Suddenly she jumped up. She had seen something. Two green lights were shining, deep in the dark. They were eyes.

'Look, Pa, look!' Laura said. 'A **wolf**!'

Pa moved quickly. He took his gun from the wagon and was ready to shoot at those green eyes. Pa threw some wood at the animal. The green eyes went close to the ground. Pa held the gun ready. The animal did not move.

'Don't shoot, Charles,' Ma said. But Pa walked slowly toward those eyes. And slowly along the ground the eyes moved toward him. And then Laura saw a little brown animal. She screamed and Pa shouted.

The next thing she knew, a happy, jumping Jack was on top of her. Her face and hands were wet from his warm wet tongue. He jumped from Pa to Ma and back to her again. Then he lay down close to Laura and slept.

When Laura went to bed that night, she looked at the large, shining stars in the sky. Pa could reach them, she thought. Suddenly she was very surprised. The largest star smiled at her!

Then she was waking up the next morning.

pork pig meat

cornbread a kind of salty cake

prairie flat, grassy land

wolf (*plural* **wolves**) a wild animal that looks like a large dog and lives in groups

READING CHECK

Tick the boxes to complete the sentences.

a The story begins when . . .

  1 ☑ Laura's family leaves Wisconsin.

  2 ☐ Pa sees animals looking at him in the forest.

  3 ☐ the ice breaks on the Mississippi River.

b Ma and Pa put . . . into the wagon.

  1 ☐ beds, tables and chairs

  2 ☐ Pa's gun and his fiddle

  3 ☐ their dog Jack

c They say goodbye to . . .

  1 ☐ nobody.

  2 ☐ their old house.

  3 ☐ their family.

d They cross the Mississippi River . . .

  1 ☐ before the ice on it breaks.

  2 ☐ when the ice on it is breaking.

  3 ☐ after the ice on it has broken.

e When they cross the creek in Kansas . . .

  1 ☐ their horses disappear.

  2 ☐ Ma gets into the water.

  3 ☐ their dog disappears.

f When they are eating supper . . .

  1 ☐ they see a wolf's eyes in the night.

  2 ☐ their dog Jack comes back.

  3 ☐ they look up at the stars in the night sky.

WORD WORK

Use the words in the wagon to complete the sentences.

cornbread
camp
settlers
Indians

canvas
pork
creek
prairie
wolves

Ma
fiddle
reins
~~Pa~~

a ......Pa....... is a short name for a father.

b .... is a short name for a mother.

c In the 1800s many North American .... went to live in the west of the country.

d .... is meat that comes from a pig.

e The top of a wagon is made of ....

f When you go on a two day journey through wild country, you must find a good place to .... for the night.

g Pa sometimes plays the ....

h Pa pulls the horses' .... to make them cross the ....

i Flat grassy land in the American West is called ....

j When you don't have time to make real bread, ... is quick to make.

k .... lived in North America before white people arrived there.

l .... are like wild dogs. They live together in groups.

GUESS WHAT

In the next chapter, Pa builds a house. What do you think happens? Tick three boxes.

a ☐ Pa cuts down trees.

b ☐ Pa hurts his hand.

c ☐ Ma hurts her foot.

d ☐ A neighbour helps.

e ☐ A neighbour makes problems.

f ☐ Laura feels afraid in the house.

Chapter 2

Pa builds the little house

It was still dark, and Pa was packing everything into the wagon. Mary and Laura ate their breakfast in a hurry. When the sun came up, they were driving across the prairie again. There was no road now. So Pet and Patty walked through the tall grass.

Before **noon**, Pa stopped the wagon. 'Here we are, Caroline!' he said. 'We'll build our house right here.'

Laura and Mary jumped out. There was nothing around them but grass that reached to the edge of the sky.

Nearby was a creek. It lay below the prairie, but they could see the dark green tree-tops. Far away another line of different greens lay across the prairie.

'That's the Verdigris River,' Pa said to Ma.

Then Pa and Ma took everything out of the wagon and put it on the ground. They took the canvas off the wagon and covered all their things. Then Pa took his **axe** and drove away.

'Where's Pa going?' Laura asked.

'To get **logs** from the creek for our house,' Ma said.

It was strange and frightening to be without the wagon on the High Prairie. The land and the sky seemed too large, and Laura felt small. She wanted to hide in the tall grass like a prairie chicken. But she didn't. First she helped Ma make the beds under the canvas cover. Then she went for a walk.

She found a mysterious little **path** in the grass, and she followed it slowly. But suddenly she felt afraid and hurried back to Ma.

When Pa returned with the logs, Laura told him about the path. 'I saw it earlier,' he said. 'It's an old **trail**, I guess.'

'When will I see a papoose?' she asked.

noon midday; twelve o'clock

axe something that is used to cut down trees or cut wood

log a long, round piece of wood that has come from a tree

path a way across a piece of land

trail a road across wild country

8

'I don't know, Laura,' Pa replied. 'You only see Indians when they want you to see them.'

Day after day Pa drove to the creek. When he had enough logs, he measured the shape of the house on the ground by walking from side to side and front to back. He dug shallow **trenches** along two sides and **rolled** two big logs into them. Then he put two strong logs across the first two to make a square. With his axe he made a deep wide cut near the end of each log. The four logs fit together at these cuts. These four strong logs could hold up the new house.

All by himself Pa built the house three logs high. Then Ma helped him. Log by log, they built the walls higher while Laura played in the tall grass. One day she heard Pa shout, 'Caroline, be careful! Get out of the way!'

A big log was falling towards Ma. Pa couldn't stop it. It crashed down, and Ma fell to the ground.

Laura and Pa ran to Ma. The log was on her foot. Pa lifted it and Ma pulled out her foot. Pa felt her leg; nothing was broken. 'Can you move your arms?' he asked. 'Can you turn your head?'

trench a long, narrow hole in the ground

roll to move something by turning it over and over

9

Ma moved her arms and turned her head. 'I'm all right,' she whispered.

'Thank God,' Pa said. 'Nothing's broken. It's only a bad **sprain**.'

Ma's face was gray but she said bravely, 'Well, a sprain will soon get better. Don't worry, Charles.'

But Ma's foot didn't get better for some time.

'The house must wait,' said Pa.

Then one afternoon, Pa came up the creek road singing.

'Good news!' he shouted. 'We have a neighbour only three kilometres away on the other side of the creek. I met him while I was **hunting**. He's going to help me finish our house, and then I'll go over and help him with his house.'

Early the next morning Mr Edwards arrived. He was tall and wore old clothes, but he was very polite to Ma. And he was a fast worker. In one day he and Pa finished the walls. They laughed and sang while they worked, and their axes made the wood fly. They cut holes for a door and two windows, and soon the house was finished except for the roof and floor.

Laura ran inside the new house. It smelled sweetly of cut wood and prairie grass. The sun shone through the window holes and fell across Laura's hands and her arms and her feet. The walls were thick and the house felt large and strong.

Ma had cooked a good supper and she and Pa invited Mr Edwards to stay. There was **rabbit** and hot cornbread with pork and even coffee with real sugar. Then Pa took out his fiddle. Mr Edwards lay on the ground near the fire to listen as Pa played Laura and Mary's favourite song, 'I am a **Gypsy** King'. Pa's voice was deeper than an old **frog's**. Laura could not stop laughing.

Then Mr Edwards jumped up and began to dance wildly in the moonlight. Pa played song after song while Mr Edwards danced. Laura's and Mary's hands were **clapping** and their feet were moving with the music, too. And Baby Carrie, who

sprain when you hurt a part of your body by suddenly turning it the wrong way

hunt to look for animals and birds in order to kill them

rabbit a small animal with long ears and big front teeth that lives in a hole in the ground

gypsy someone who does not like to stay in the same place for a long time

frog a small green animal that lives near water and has long back legs for jumping

clap to hit your hands together in time with music or to show that you like something

had woken up, was sitting in Ma's arms, clapping her little hands and laughing.

When it was time for Mr Edwards to go, he took his gun and said good night. Pa played one last song as Mr Edwards walked away into the darkness, singing happily. When the song ended, the prairie was silent. Only the wind whispered in the tall grass.

❋ ❋ ❋

'The walls are up,' Pa said to Ma the next morning. Let's move in. I heard wolves everywhere around us last night. We should have strong thick walls around us. I'll make the floor and roof later because I must build a **stable** for Pet and Patty as fast as I can. They should be safe inside walls, too.'

'Why haven't we seen any Indians?' Ma asked.

'I don't know,' Pa replied. 'I've seen the places where they camp. They're away hunting for food now, I guess.'

After breakfast Pa got on top of the walls to put the canvas wagon cover over the house. The canvas blew wildly in the wind, and so did Pa's hair. Once he almost flew away into the air like a big bird. But he finally tied the canvas down.

By dinner time, the house was ready. The beds were made on the floor. Short logs had become chairs. Pa's gun was up in its place over the door. It was a pleasant house.

'Before winter comes I'll make a wood floor and a solid roof,' Pa said. 'But that must wait until I finish helping Mr Edwards and building a stable. We're going to do well here, Caroline. We'll be happy here for the rest of our lives.'

Laura liked this place, too. She liked the great big sky, the winds, and the wide land. Everything was so clean and big and wonderful.

Inside the thick walls of their new home they felt warm and safe. Pa put up a **quilt** over the door hole. As she fell asleep that night, Laura heard a wolf's cry from somewhere far away on the prairie. She did not feel so frightened.

stable a building for horses to sleep in at night or live in during the winter

quilt a warm thick cover for a bed that is made with many pieces of colourful cloth

READING CHECK

Put the sentences in the correct order. Number them 1–11.

a ☐ Pa digs trenches.

b ☐ Pa measures the shape of the house on the ground.

c ☐ They have supper with Mr Edwards.

d ☐ Pa rolls logs into the trenches.

e ☐ 1 Pa goes with his axe to get logs from the creek.

f ☐ Ma helps Pa to build the walls.

g ☐ They move into the house.

h ☐ They cut holes for a door and windows in the walls.

i ☐ Mr Edwards comes to help Pa build the walls.

j ☐ Pa puts a canvas roof on the house.

k ☐ A log falls on Ma's foot.

WORD WORK

1 **Complete these sentences using the correct form of the words from Chapter 2.**

a Pa uses an a x e to cut down trees.

b The house on the prairie is made of l _ _ _.

c Pa sings a song about a g _ _ _ _.

d He sounds like a f _ _ _.

e Pa puts up a q _ _ _ _ over the door.

f Sometimes Pa catches a r _ _ _ _ _ for supper.

g When he is ready to build the house, Pa digs a t _ _ _ _ _ _.

ACTIVITIES

2 Find words in the river to complete these sentences.

claphuntnoonrollsprainstabletrail

a Indians sometimes travel on an old Indian $\underline{trail}$ near the house.

b Pa builds a _ _ _ _ _ _ for the horses.

c Ma doesn't break her leg; it's only a _ _ _ _ _ _.

d When Pa sings Laura and Mary _ _ _ _ in time with the music.

e _ _ _ _ is in the middle of the day.

f Pa and Mr Edwards sometimes _ _ _ _ together.

g The best way to move heavy logs is to _ _ _ _ them.

GUESS WHAT

In the next chapter, some wolves frighten the family. What do you think happens? Tick the boxes.

a The wolves …

   1 ☐ kill and eat Pa.

   2 ☐ attack Pa.

   3 ☐ circle the house.

b Pa …

   1 ☐ meets some wolves on the prairie.

   2 ☐ shoots some wolves.

   3 ☐ makes friends with a wolf.

c Laura …

   1 ☐ climbs a tree to escape.

   2 ☐ hears the wolves at night.

   3 ☐ thinks that the wolves are dogs.

d Ma …

   1 ☐ puts the girls to bed as usual.

   2 ☐ brings Pet and Patty into the house.

   3 ☐ wants to go back to Wisconsin.

13

Chapter 3 🐾

Wolves frighten the family

Pa and Mr Edwards built the stable for Pet and Patty in one day. By the time they put the roof on, it was dark. 'Now!' said Pa. 'Let those wolves **howl**! I'll sleep tonight.'

In the morning when Laura went into the stable, she found a surprise waiting for her. A little **colt** with long ears stood beside Pet! When Laura ran toward it, gentle Pet put back her ears and showed her teeth.

'Stay back, Laura!' Pa shouted. 'She could bite you.' Then he said to Pet, 'You know we won't hurt your baby, Pet.' Pet let Pa touch the baby, but she didn't let Laura or Mary go near her.

Early that afternoon, Pa rode Patty across the prairie to see what he could see. There was plenty of meat in the house, so he did not take his gun.

By late afternoon, he still had not come home. Ma and Laura began to get supper ready outside by the fire. Mary was in the house, taking care of the baby, and Laura asked Ma, 'What's the matter with Jack?'

Jack was walking up and down and around the house, looking worried. His hair stood up on his neck. Then Pet started running around in circles.

Ma looked around at the wide prairie and the sky but didn't see anything unusual. 'It's probably nothing at all, Laura,' Ma said. She made the coffee. The prairie chicken that was cooking on the fire began to smell good. But all the time Ma went on looking around.

Suddenly Patty came running fast across the prairie. Pa was almost flat, holding onto her neck. Patty ran past the stable before Pa could stop her. She was **trembling**, and her black

howl to make a long, loud, high crying noise like a wolf or a dog

colt a young horse

tremble to shake with fear

coat was hot and wet. Pa was hot and tired, too.

'What's the matter, Charles?' Ma asked him.

Pa's eyes were looking toward the creek, so Ma and Laura looked at it, too. But they only saw grass and trees.

'What is it?' Ma asked again. 'Why were you riding Patty so fast?'

'I was afraid the wolves had come here.'

'Wolves!' Ma cried. 'What wolves?'

'Everything's fine now, Caroline,' said Pa. 'Let me rest a minute.'

Then he said, 'We saw fifty of them, Caroline. They were the biggest wolves I've ever seen. It was terrible.'

Supper was ready. Mary and Laura stayed close to the fire and kept Baby Carrie with them. They could feel the darkness everywhere, and they didn't stop looking around. Shadows moved on the prairie. Jack did not **growl**, but his ears were lifted, listening to the darkness. The girls ate their chicken as they listened to Pa telling Ma about the wolves.

He had found some more neighbours. Settlers were coming in and building houses along both sides of the creek. Not far away, a man and his wife were building a house. Their name was Scott, and Pa said they were nice people. As he was riding home across the prairie, a **pack** of wolves came out of nowhere. They were all around Pa in a moment.

'It was a big pack,' Pa said. 'There were fifty wolves, and the biggest wolves I ever saw in my life. Their **leader** was a meter tall. I tell you, my hair stood straight up.'

'And you didn't have your gun,' said Ma.

'I know. But to be honest, I didn't miss it. You can't fight fifty wolves with one gun.'

'What did you do?' Ma asked.

'Nothing,' said Pa. 'Patty tried to run, but I pulled the reins hard and made her walk. Wolves will chase and hurt a running horse.'

growl to make a long, deep, angry sound (like a dog)

pack a group (of wolves or dogs)

leader the most important one in a group

'How awful, Charles!' Ma said quietly.

'Yes, it was,' said Pa. 'Those wolves just walked along with us, like a pack of dogs going along with a horse. They were all around us, jumping and playing with each other, just like dogs. We were lucky they weren't hungry.'

Laura's mouth and eyes were wide open. Her heart was beating fast.

'Patty was trembling all over,' Pa said. 'She was so scared. I was, too. But I made her walk. When we got near the creek, the leader turned down toward the creek, and the rest of the pack followed him. That's when I let Patty go. I was scared the whole way home. I thought the wolves might come this way. I knew you could keep the wolves out of the house with the gun. But Pet and her colt were outside.'

'I guess I could save our horses, Charles,' Ma said.

'I know,' said Pa. 'I wasn't thinking straight. But the wolves are far from here by now, and all's well that ends well.'

Jack was walking around the campfire. When he stopped to smell the air, the hair lifted on his neck.

'It's time for bed, girls!' Ma said. She took them all into the house. But it took Laura a long time to fall asleep.

Suddenly she was sitting straight up in bed. She had been asleep. Light from the moon was coming through the window and the **cracks** in the wall. Pa was standing there with his gun.

Suddenly, a wolf howled right in Laura's ear.

She pulled away from the wall. The wolf was just on the other side of it. Laura was too scared to speak. Then many wolves started howling all around the house, and Laura got out of bed. Pa turned his head and saw her standing there.

'Do you want to see them, Laura?' he asked, softly.

Without saying anything Laura walked over to Pa. He put down his gun and lifted her up to the window. There in the light of the moon sat a half circle of wolves. They looked at

crack a very
narrow space
between two things

16

Laura, and she looked at them. The biggest one was taller than Laura. His coat was gray and his eyes were shining and green. Laura looked and looked at that wolf.

'He's awfully big,' Laura said into Pa's ear.

'Yes, and see how his coat shines,' Pa said into her hair. 'They're in a circle around the house.'

Laura went with him to the other window. There she saw the other half of the circle of wolves. The big wolf lifted his nose to the sky and howled. All the other wolves answered him. The noise filled the wide prairie.

'Now go back to bed, Laura,' Pa said. 'Go to sleep. Jack and I will take care of you all.'

So Laura went back to bed. She heard the wolves howling and trying to smell them through the cracks in the walls of the house. It was a long time before she fell asleep.

READING CHECK

1 Correct ten more mistakes in the chapter summary.

Pet

The day after Pa and Mr Edwards build a stable for the horses, ~~Patty~~ has a baby. Only

Ma can touch her baby, not Laura or Mary. One evening Ma is cooking a prairie chicken

when Pa comes walking home on Patty after a day away. Patty is happy, and hot and

wet because she has seen some wolves out on the prairie. Pa tells Ma about the wolves

and about some terrible neighbours called Scott whom he has met. On his way home

he suddenly finds there are five wolves all around him and he has his gun with him. Pa

makes Patty run so the wolves do not attack her. They jump and play next to Patty. When

the wolves go after their leader down to the creek, Patty runs home fast with Pa on her

back. That afternoon the wolves sit in a circle around the house and Laura sees the

leader with his black coat and red eyes.

2 Match the first and second parts of these sentences.

a Pa doesn't take his gun with him . . .

b Ma cooks outside . . .

c Jack and Pet move about worriedly . . .

d The wolves don't eat Pa and Patty . . .

e The hair on Jack's neck lifts . . .

f Laura is very scared . . .

1 because they aren't hungry.

2 because there's plenty of meat in the house.

3 because the house doesn't have a chimney.

4 because he can smell the wolves coming nearer.

5 because there's a wolf just on the other side of the wall from her.

6 because they can hear Patty running from far away.

WORD WORK

Correct the boxed words in these sentences. They all come from Chapter 3.

a Laura hears the **bowl** of a wolf outside the house. ...howl......

b Wolves often move from place to place in **parks** . ...

c Pet has a little **bolt** . ...

d Laura can hear the wolves through **tracks** in the wall. ....

e When Patty sees wolves she **crumbles** . ...

f The **lender** of the wolves is very big. ....

g Jack the dog listens quietly to noises from the prairie and doesn't **prowl** .
....

GUESS WHAT

Pa finishes the house in the next chapter. What do you think he makes?
Tick the boxes.

a ☐ a door
b ☐ a chimney
c ☐ a roof
d ☐ a toilet
e ☐ stairs
f ☐ a floor

Chapter 4 🏠

Pa finishes the house

saw a metal knife with teeth that is used to cut wood

board a flat piece of wood for building things

frame the piece of wood around the outside of a door or a picture

hinge the thing which fastens a door to its frame

When Laura woke up the next morning, the warm sun was on her face. She ran outdoors. Mary was talking to Ma by the fire. There were no wolves anywhere. Pa came up the creek road with his gun in hand. He had made sure that the wolves were gone.

They all sat by the fire and ate their breakfast. 'I'll make a door today,' Pa said. 'I want more than a quilt between us and the wolves next time.'

After breakfast, Pa took the horses and his axe and went to get wood for the door. Mary watched, but Laura helped Pa to make the door. She gave him his **saw**, which he used to cut the logs at the ends. With his axe he made nice straight

boards from the logs. He laid the long boards on the ground and fastened some shorter boards across them. That made the door. Then Pa made a door **frame** and put **hinges** on the door to make it open and close. While he put the door in place, Laura stood against it to hold it up, and Pa fastened the hinges to the frame.

When the door was finished, it was beautiful and strong. 'Now we're all safe!' said Pa. 'And I had a fine little helper!' He put his hand gently on Laura's head. The sun was going down, the wind was cooler, and supper was cooking on the fire. It was salt pork, which made the best supper smells that Laura had ever smelled.

That night Pa said to Ma, 'Now, Caroline, I'm going to build you a **fireplace**. Then you can do your cooking inside the house. I've never seen such a sunny place as this, but I suppose that one of these days the rains will come.'

'Yes, Charles,' Ma said. 'Good weather always comes to an end, sooner or later.'

❄ ❄ ❄

And so Pa was soon cutting away the grass just outside the wall of the house where he was going to build the fireplace. Then he climbed into the wagon. He looked down at Laura; she was looking up at him. 'Do you want to go along, Laura? You and Mary?'

Ma said that they could. The girls climbed up and sat on the high seat beside Pa. Pet and Patty started with a little jump and pulled the wagon down the new road that Pa's wagon wheels had begun to make.

They rode through dry valleys and over low, round hills. Forests covered some of these hills, but some of them were open and grassy. **Deer** were lying under the trees or standing and eating grass in the sun. They lifted their heads and watched the wagon with their large, soft eyes. Birds sang and rabbits jumped out of the way of the wagon.

When they arrived at the creek, Pa said, 'You girls can play, but don't go too far into the water.'

So Laura and Mary played by the creek while Pa dug the big rocks that he needed for the fireplace. When the wagon was full, they rode home to the High Prairie, where the wind was blowing and the grass was singing. Laura decided she liked the High Prairie best. It was so wide and sweet and clean.

That afternoon, the family watched Pa build the fireplace. First, he had cleared grass in a square outside the house wall. Now he put a row of rocks around the square. Next he mixed

fireplace a place in the house where you can have a fire

deer a large wild animal that can run fast

earth and water to a beautiful, thick **mud**. He put some mud over the rocks. In the mud he put another row of rocks. With rocks and mud and more rocks and more mud, Pa built the fireplace and chimney as high as the house wall. Then he used wood and mud to finish the top of the chimney. Finally he went into the house, and with his axe and saw he cut a hole in the wall. And there was the fireplace!

The whole family stood and **admired** it. Ma carefully built a little fire in the new fireplace and cooked a prairie chicken for supper. And that evening they ate in their house. The chicken tasted so good in Laura's mouth. Her hands and face were washed and her hair was brushed. She sat up straight on her log chair and used her knife and fork nicely, as Ma had taught her. She did not say anything, because children must not speak at the table until they are spoken to, but she looked at Pa and Ma and Mary and Baby Carrie, and she felt happy. It was nice to be in a house again.

❋ ❋ ❋

All day long, every day, Laura and Mary were busy. When the dishes were washed and the beds were made, there was always

earth the ground is made of this

mud soft, wet earth

admire to look at something and think that it is very good

plenty to do and to see. In the tall grass, they looked for birds and watched baby prairie chickens running to their mothers. They watched **snakes** lying still in the sun or moving fast through the prairie. All the time, of course, either Laura or Mary was taking care of Baby Carrie. Sometimes Laura forgot to be quiet when Baby Carrie was sleeping. She ran around and shouted until Ma came to the door and said, 'Laura, dear, must you shout like an Indian? In fact, you girls are getting as brown as Indians in the sun! Why can't you learn to keep your hats on?'

'Pa, when are we going to see a papoose?' Laura asked. Pa was up on the house wall, beginning to put on the roof.

'Why do you want to see an Indian baby?' Ma said, surprised. 'Put on your hat and forget your crazy ideas.'

But Laura did not forget the papoose. This was Indian country and she wanted to see Indians. She knew that she would see them sometime, but she was tired of waiting.

Pa had taken the canvas off the top of the house. For days he had been carrying logs from the creeks and cutting them into long, thin boards. The boards were lying all around the house.

Now Pa reached down and pulled up a board. He put it across the **rafters**. Then he began to **nail** the board to the rafters. Pa pulled up and nailed down more boards, all the way to the top of the rafters. The roof was done. Rain would never get in. Then Pa made a floor with beautiful hard wood.

'You've done a wonderful job, Charles,' Ma said.

They were all happy that night. The sky was full of stars. Pa sat for a long time by the open door and played his fiddle and sang to his family in the house, and to the stars outside.

Later Pa dug a **well** with Mr Scott's help and they didn't need to fetch muddy water from the creek any more. And after that he went to town to get glass to put in the windows, and then the house was truly finished.

snake a long animal with no legs

rafter a piece of wood under a roof that helps to hold it up

nail to fasten one thing to another thing (with a thick metal pin)

well a deep hole in the ground where people can get water

READING CHECK

Are these sentences true or false? Tick the boxes.

		True	False
a	Mary helps Pa to make the door.	☐	☑
b	Laura and Mary see deer and rabbits on their way to the creek.	☐	☐
c	Laura and Mary help Pa to dig rocks from the creek.	☐	☐
d	The family watch Pa build a fireplace.	☐	☐
e	Laura shouts like an Indian and is as brown as an Indian, too.	☐	☐
f	Ma likes her daughters getting brown in the sun.	☐	☐
g	Ma is very happy with all Pa's work on the house.	☐	☐

WORD WORK

1 Write the words to match the pictures.

a s a w

b w _ _ _

c s _ _ _ _

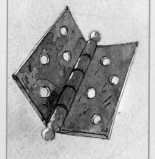

d d _ _ _

e h _ _ _ _

f f _ _ _ _ _ _ _ _

2 Find words in Chapter 4 to match the definitions.

a the ground is made of this *earth*

b a long flat piece of wood _ _ _ _ _

c long pieces of wood that hold up a roof _ _ _ _ _ _ _ _

d wet earth _ _ _

e this holds something in it like a door or a picture _ _ _ _ _

f to think that something is very good _ _ _ _ _ _

g to use a metal pin to fasten things together _ _ _ _

GUESS WHAT

**Laura finally sees Indians in
the next chapter. What do
you think happens? Tick three
boxes.**

a ☐ Laura finds an Indian
baby.

b ☐ Indians come to visit
Laura's house.

c ☐ Jack attacks the Indians.

d ☐ An Indian kills Jack.

e ☐ Laura goes to an Indian
camp.

f ☐ Laura finds something
nice made by the Indians.

Chapter 5

Indians!

Early one morning Pa took his gun and went hunting. Jack wanted to go, too, but Pa tied him to the stable.

'No, Jack,' Pa said. 'You must stay here and take care of the family.' Then he said to Mary and Laura, 'Don't untie him, girls.'

Poor Jack lay down. Mary and Laura stayed by the stable all morning and tried to play with him, but he was miserable. Jack's head was on Laura's leg and she was talking to him when he suddenly stood up and growled. The hair on his neck stood straight up and his eyes stared, red and angry.

Laura was afraid. Jack had never growled at her before. Then she looked over her shoulder, where Jack was looking, and she saw two wild men, one behind the other coming closer on the Indian trail.

'Mary! Look!' she shouted. Mary looked and saw them, too.

They were tall, thin, **fierce**-looking men. Their skin was reddish-brown. Their eyes were black and shining. There were **feathers** on their heads.

'Indians!' Mary whispered. Laura suddenly felt cold. Her legs trembled. Jack growled angrily.

The Indians came closer and closer. Then Mary and Laura watched them walk right into the house! Jack was growling, jumping, and trying to break free.

'Jack's here,' Laura whispered to Mary. 'We'll be safe if we stay close to him.'

'But they're in the house,' Mary whispered. 'They're in the house with Ma and Carrie!'

Then Laura began to shake all over. She knew she must do something. What were the Indians doing to Ma and Baby

fierce very strong and frightening

feathers birds have these on their bodies to keep them warm and to help them fly

Carrie? There was no sound from the house.

'Oh, what are they doing to Ma?' Laura screamed, in a whisper.

'Oh, I don't know!' Mary whispered.

'I'm going to untie Jack,' Laura whispered loudly. 'He'll kill them.'

'Pa told us not to do that,' Mary answered.

'He didn't know Indians would come,' Laura said.

'He said not to untie Jack,' Mary was almost crying.

Laura thought of little Baby Carrie and Ma, there in the house with those Indians. 'I'm going in to help Ma!' she said.

She ran two steps and then turned and flew back to Jack. She hid her face against his neck.

'We mustn't leave Ma in there alone,' Mary whispered. She stood still and trembled.

Laura made herself leave Jack. She shut her eyes and ran towards the house as fast as she could. She fell down and her eyes opened. She got up again and started running. Mary was right behind her. They came to the door. It was open, and they entered the house without a sound.

The **naked** wild men stood by the fireplace. Ma was cooking something over the fire while Baby Carrie hid her face in Ma's dress. Laura ran towards Ma, but as she reached the Indians, she smelled something awful. She looked up at the Indians and ran to hide behind the table. With one eye, she looked out at the wild men.

First, she saw the **moccasins** on their feet. Then their thin, red-brown legs, all the way up. Around their **waists** each Indian wore the skin of a small animal. The skin was black and white, and now Laura knew what had made that smell. The skins were made from fresh **skunks**. There was a knife and a small axe in each skin.

Their faces were very calm and very fierce. These wild men had no hair around their ears, where hair usually grows. There

naked without clothes

moccasins soft shoes made of animal skins

waist the middle of the body

skunk a small black and white animal that makes a bad smell when it is frightened

was hair only at the very top of their heads, and they had put feathers in it.

When Laura looked out from behind the table, both Indians were looking straight at her. Her heart jumped. The Indians did not move. Only their eyes shone. Laura did not move, either.

Then the Indians made short sounds like 'Hah!' Laura hid again behind the table. She heard them sitting down on the floor. She heard Ma giving them cornbread and she heard them eating it. When Laura looked again, she saw they had eaten every bit of the cornbread. Then the Indians got up. They looked at Ma, made deep noises in their **throats**, and walked out the door. Their feet made no sound at all.

Ma sat down on the bed. She looked sick. She put her arms around Laura and Mary.

'Do you feel sick, Ma?' Mary asked her.

'No,' said Ma. 'I'm just thankful they're gone.'

Soon Pa arrived home with a big rabbit and two prairie chickens. He put his gun up in its place over the door. Laura

throat the inside of your neck

and Mary threw their arms around him, both talking at the same time.

'What's all this?' he said. 'Indians? So you've seen Indians at last, have you, Laura? I noticed they have a **camp** in a valley west of here. Did Indians come into the house, Caroline?'

'Yes, Charles, two of them,' Ma said. 'I'm sorry, but they took all your **tobacco** and ate a lot of cornbread. I just gave them what they wanted. Oh, Charles! I was afraid!'

'You did the right thing,' Pa told her. 'We don't want to make enemies of the Indians.' Then he said, 'What a smell!'

'They wore fresh skunk skins around their waists,' said Ma. 'And that was all they wore.'

Later, when Laura and Mary were helping Pa clean the prairie chickens, Laura said, 'I wanted to untie Jack to eat those Indians.'

Pa laid down his knife and asked in a terrible voice, 'Did you girls even think of untying Jack?'

Laura dropped her head and whispered, 'Yes, Pa.'

'After I told you not to?' Pa said, in a more terrible voice.

'Yes, Pa,' Mary whispered, almost crying.

For a moment Pa was silent.

'After this,' he then said in his angry voice, 'you girls must do as I say. You must always obey me. Do you hear?'

'Yes, Pa,' Laura and Mary whispered.

'If the Indians come again and Jack is untied, he'll bite them. And then there will be trouble. Bad trouble. Do you understand?'

'Yes, Pa,' the girls said. But they did not understand.

'Do as you're told,' said Pa, 'and you'll be safe.'

✷ ✷ ✷

One day Pa said that the Indians had left their little camp on the prairie. 'Do you want to see it?' he asked Laura and Mary. When the girls jumped up and down with excitement, Pa said, 'Come on then, let's go.'

camp a place where people live in tents for a short time

tobacco the dry leaves that are smoked in cigarettes

The ground was hot under their feet. They went farther and farther into the big prairie. At last they went down into the little valley where the Indians had camped. Laura and Mary looked around. There were small animals, flowers, and trees. It was a beautiful secret place.

'Pa, are there other Indian camps on the prairie?' Laura asked.

'Yes, Laura,' he answered.

'Are there Indians in them?' she whispered.

'I don't know,' said Pa. 'Perhaps.'

She held one of his hands and Mary held the other, and together they looked at the Indians' camp. There were old campfires. They could see where Indian horses had eaten the grass, where big and small moccasins had walked, and where Indians had cooked and eaten.

Suddenly Laura shouted, 'Look! Look!' Something bright blue was shining on the ground. She picked it up. It was a beautiful blue **bead**. Laura shouted with excitement.

Then Mary saw a red bead, and Laura saw a green one, and they forgot everything except beads. They found white beads and brown beads, and more and more red and blue beads. All that afternoon they looked for beads. When they had finished, the sun was going down. Laura had a handful of beads, and so did Mary. Pa put them carefully in his pockets, and they all went home together.

Supper was cooking on the fire when they arrived, and Baby Carrie was playing on the floor. 'Sorry we're late!' said Pa, and then he took the beads out of his pockets and showed them to Ma. 'But look what the girls found,' he said.

'Oh, they're beautiful!' Ma said with a smile.

bead a small, round piece of glass or wood that you can wear on a string around your neck

Laura thought the beads looked even prettier than before. She touched her beads with her finger and watched them shine. 'These are mine,' she said.

Then Mary said, 'Carrie can have mine.'

Ma waited for Laura to speak. But Laura didn't want to say anything. She felt all hot inside and wished that Mary wasn't always such a good girl. But she couldn't let Mary be better than she was.

necklace
something pretty
that you wear
around your neck

So she said, slowly, 'Carrie can have mine, too.'

'You're good little girls,' Ma said. She put Mary's beads into Mary's hands, and Laura's into Laura's hands, and she said, 'You can make a pretty **necklace** for Carrie to wear around her neck.'

Mary and Laura sat side by side on their bed and made Carrie's necklace. They didn't say anything. Perhaps Mary felt sweet and good inside, but Laura didn't. When she looked at Mary she wanted to hit her. So she didn't look at her again.

The beads made a beautiful necklace. Carrie laughed when she saw it. Then Ma tied it around Carrie's little neck and Laura felt a little bit better. It looked so pretty on her.

But when Carrie felt the beads on her neck, she tried to break the necklace. So Ma untied it and put it away.

'Carrie can wear it when she's older,' Ma said.

Laura still wanted those pretty beads for herself. But she knew it had been a wonderful day. She knew she was never going to forget the Indian camp.

READING CHECK

Match the sentences with the people.

Ma

Pa

Baby Carrie

Laura

Mary

a . . . doesn't want the girls to untie Jack.

b Laura and . . . go into the house after the Indians.

c . . . cooks something for the Indians to eat.

d . . . hides her face in Ma's dress.

e . . . hides from the Indians behind the table.

f . . . looks sick when the Indians have gone.

g The Indians take all of . . .'s tobacco.

h . . . doesn't want to make enemies of the Indians.

i . . . and Mary find some beads in an empty Indian camp.

j . . . doesn't want to keep her beads.

k . . . wants to keep her beads.

l In the end both girls make a necklace from the beads for . . .

WORD WORK

Use the words below to complete the sentences.

beads
camps naked
feathers necklaces
fierce skunks
moccasins tobacco

a Crazy Horse was a very ...fierce..... Indian chief.

b Cigarettes are made from ....

c Indian children often ran about .... because they didn't like wearing clothes.

d Indian shoes are called ....

e Indians often wore .... in their hair.

f Because Indians moved to different places in summer and winter they lived in ....

g Indian men and women wore .... round their necks.

h Laura and Mary found lots of coloured .... on the ground.

i .... are smelly black and white animals.

GUESS WHAT

Match the first and second parts of these sentences to find out what happens in the next chapter.

a Pa works happily moving cows for a day but . . .

b Pa works for a second day and . . .

c First Laura gets ill and . . .

d A doctor comes and . . .

e A neighbour, Mrs Scott, comes and . . .

1 then the whole family gets ill.

2 gives Laura some medicine.

3 gets very dirty and tired.

4 cares for the whole family.

5 is paid with two cows and some meat.

Chapter 6

Summertime on the prairie

Summer had come to the prairie, and the air was still and warm. One evening Laura and Pa were sitting outside under a big moon while Pa played his fiddle. Everything was so beautiful. Laura wanted it to stay that way for ever. Suddenly she heard a strange, low sound far away. 'What's that?' she asked.

Pa listened. '**Cattle**!' he said. 'It must be the cattle **herds** going north.' They listened together and Laura thought she could hear a song.

'Is that singing, Pa?' she asked.

'Yes,' Pa said. 'The **cowboys** are singing to their cattle. It's time for them to sleep, and you too!'

The next morning when Laura ran out of the house, two strange men were sitting on horses by the stable. They were talking to Pa. They were as red-brown as Indians, and they wore big, wide hats and cowboy boots. **Handkerchiefs** were tied around their necks, and guns were at their sides. They said goodbye to Pa and rode away across the hot prairie.

'What a piece of luck!' Pa said to Ma. 'Those men are cowboys. They want me to help them to move the cattle across the creek. They'll pay me with **beef**. How would you like a good piece of beef?'

'Oh, Charles!' Ma said, and her eyes shone.

Pa tied his biggest handkerchief around his neck. He showed Laura how a cowboy pulls it up over his mouth and nose to keep the **dust** out. Then Pa rode Patty down the Indian trail. All day the sun shone hot and the sound of cattle herds came nearer. Laura and Mary could see the dust that they made.

cattle a number of cows

herd a group of animals that lives and eats together, like cattle

cowboy someone who takes care of cattle

handkerchief something that you use to dry your nose or eyes

beef the meat from a cow

dust very small pieces of dry earth

Pa came riding home as the sun was going down, covered with dust. There was dust in his hair and around his eyes, and dust fell from his clothes. He was going to work again the next day because the cattle were not across the creek yet. The cattle moved slowly, eating grass as they went.

Pa fell asleep soon after supper that night. Laura lay awake and listened to the sounds of the cattle on the prairie and the high, lonely songs of the cowboys. The songs sounded like the crying of wolves under the moon, and they made Laura feel sad.

All the next day, Laura and Mary watched the prairie. Suddenly out of the dusty grass, not far from the stable, cattle came running.

They ran fast, their feet beating the ground. A cowboy on a black-and-white horse rode faster to get in front of them. He waved his big hat and shouted at the cattle as he moved them along. They all went over a low hill and disappeared.

Laura ran around outside, waving her hat and shouting wildly.

'Laura,' Ma said. 'Stop that! A young lady shouldn't shout like that.'

'I wish I could be a cowboy, Ma,' Laura said.

Late that afternoon, Laura saw Pa riding home with two cowboys, a cow, and a little black-and-white **calf**. Pa tied the cow to the stable and said goodbye to the cowboys. Ma's eyes opened wide when she saw their new animals. 'They gave me the cow because she was too thin to sell,' Pa said when he came in the house. 'And the calf is too small to travel. They gave me the beef, too.'

Then Pa went out to the stable to get some milk from the cow for Baby Carrie. They watched her drink all that good milk. Baby Carrie's little red tongue cleaned her milky lips and she laughed.

Ma cooked the beef and everyone felt happy. Nothing had

calf a young cow

ever tasted as good as that thick, red meat. The cattle were far away now, and the girls couldn't hear the songs of the cowboys any more.

❋ ❋ ❋

A little later in the year there were **blackberries**, and in the hot afternoons Laura went with Ma to pick them in the **bushes** by the creek. There were **mosquitoes** everywhere in the blackberry bushes, and they liked to bite Laura and Ma.

Laura's fingers and her mouth got purple-black from eating the big blackberries. Her face, hands, and feet were covered with mosquito bites. But every day they brought home **buckets** full of berries, and Ma laid them out in the sun to dry.

In the day there were only a few mosquitoes in the house. But at night, if the wind wasn't blowing hard, there were lots of them. On still nights Pa burned wet grass around the house to keep the mosquitoes away, but they came just the same.

Pa could not play his fiddle in the evenings because so many mosquitoes bit him. Mr Edwards did not visit after supper, because there were too many mosquitoes in the creek. And every morning Laura's face was full of red mosquito bites.

'It'll get colder soon,' Pa said, 'and then they'll go.'

Laura did not feel very well. One day she felt cold even in the hot sun, and she could not get warm by the fire.

'Why don't you and Mary go out to play?' Ma asked Laura.

'I don't want to play,' answered Laura. 'I'm tired and I **ache**.'

Ma stopped her work. 'Where do you ache?'

'I don't know,' said Laura. 'I just ache. My legs ache.'

'I ache, too,' Mary said.

Ma put her hand against Laura's face. 'You're as hot as fire,' she said.

Laura felt like crying, but of course she didn't. Only little babies cried. 'I'm cold now,' she said. 'And my back aches.'

'Charles,' Ma called. 'Look at the girls. I think they're sick.'

blackberry a small, sweet, black fruit

bush a small tree

mosquito a small flying insect that drinks blood

bucket an open container used for carrying and holding things

ache to feel a pain

Pa and Ma put them to bed in the middle of the day. Laura did not really go to sleep, but she did not really wake up again for a long, long time. Strange things seemed to be happening. She heard voices, but no words. Sometimes she felt as cold as ice, and then she was burning. Days and nights passed like this.

She heard Pa say, 'Go to bed, Caroline.'

Ma said, 'You're sicker than I am, Charles.'

Then one day Laura opened her eyes and saw the bright light of the sun. Mary was beside her crying, 'I want a drink of water! I want a drink of water!' Jack was walking between the big bed and her little bed. Pa was lying on the floor by the big bed. Jack took Pa's shirt in his teeth and shook it. Pa's head lifted up a little, and he said, 'I must get up, I must. Caroline and the girls.' Then his head fell back and he lay still. Jack howled.

Laura tried to get up, but she was too tired. Then she saw Ma's red face looking from the big bed. Mary was still crying for water. Ma looked at Mary and then she looked at Laura, and she whispered, 'Laura, can you get up?'

'Yes, Ma.' Laura said. This time she got out of bed, but when she tried to stand up, she fell down again. She felt Jack's tongue on her face and she held onto him and sat up.

She knew she must get water for Mary, and she did. She **crawled** all the way

crawl to move along slowly with your body close to the floor

across the floor to the water bucket and then crawled all the way back to Mary with the water. Mary's eyes did not open, but her mouth drank all the water. Then she stopped crying. Laura crawled back into bed. It was a long time before she began to get warm again.

Sometimes she heard Jack howling and she thought he was a wolf. She lay in bed burning and hearing him howl. She heard the voices talking again, and she opened her eyes and saw a big, black face close to hers. Its eyes were black and soft. This face smiled, and a deep voice said softly, 'Drink this, little girl.'

Laura opened her mouth but the drink was bitter and she turned her head away. The deep voice said again, 'Drink it. It will make you well.' So she drank the bitter medicine.

When Laura woke again a fat woman was by the fire. She brought Laura water and a cup of something hot that tasted good, like chicken.

'Drink it all up, like a good child,' she said.

Laura looked at Mary asleep beside her; she looked at Pa and Ma asleep in the big bed. Jack lay half asleep on the floor. Laura looked again at the fat woman and asked, 'Who are you?'

'I'm Mrs Scott,' she said, smiling. 'I'm here to take care of everything until you're all well. Now go to sleep.'

The next morning Laura felt so much better that she wanted to get up, but Mrs Scott said she must stay in bed until the doctor came. Laura was surprised when she saw him. He was the black man! Laura had never seen a black man before, and she could not take her eyes off Dr Tan. He talked with Pa and Ma and laughed his big laugh before he hurried away.

Mrs Scott said that all the settlers along the creek were sick. She had been going from house to house, working day and night. 'You're lucky to be alive,' she said. 'It's because Dr Tan found you when he did.'

Dr Tan was a doctor with the Indians. He was on his way to the town of Independence when he passed Pa's house. Strangely Jack, who usually hated strangers, had run after Dr Tan and made him come in. 'And here you all were, more dead than alive,' Mrs Scott said. 'All of you sick at the same time. Dr Tan stayed with you a day and a night before I came. Now he's taking care of all the sick settlers.'

The next day Pa and Laura were out of bed. The next day, Ma got up, and then Mary. They were all thin and shaky, but they could take care of themselves. So Mrs Scott went home.

'How can we ever thank you?' Ma said.

'It's nothing,' Mrs Scott said. 'Neighbours are there to help each other.'

Pa was thinner and walked slowly, and Ma often sat down. Mary and Laura didn't feel like playing. But every day they got a little bit stronger. Pa couldn't work outside, so he sat in the house and made a beautiful chair for Ma. He played his fiddle, and Mary and Laura were happy.

No one knew, in those days, that the illness was **malaria**, and that it came from the mosquitoes.

malaria an illness that is brought by mosquitoes

READING CHECK

Tick the best answers.

a Why does Laura hear singing at night?
 1 ☐ Pa is singing and playing his fiddle.
 2 ☐ Ma is singing to Baby Carrie.
 3 ☑ Cowboys are singing to their cows.

b Why do the cowboys give Pa a cow and a calf?
 1 ☐ To pay him for his work.
 2 ☐ The animals are weak.
 3 ☐ There is no meat to give him.

c When do mosquitoes come in the house?
 1 ☐ When people eat blackberries.
 2 ☐ When it's windy.
 3 ☐ At night.

d How do they try to stop the mosquitoes?
 1 ☐ Mr Edwards visits after supper.
 2 ☐ Pa plays his fiddle.
 3 ☐ Pa burns wet grass.

e What happens to Laura?
 1 ☐ She is ill for a long time.
 2 ☐ She cries because she's so hot.
 3 ☐ She asks Mary for a drink of water.

f Who does Jack bring to care for the family when they are ill?
 1 ☐ Dr Tan, a doctor on his way to Independence.
 2 ☐ An Indian.
 3 ☐ Mrs Scott, a neighbour.

WORD WORK

1 Find words in the beads to complete the sentences.

a You use a h*andkerchief* to dry your nose or eyes. C I D A R H E F K H E N

b A number of cows are called c _ _ _ _ _ _ . T A C L E T

c Cows move about in a h _ _ _ . D E R H

d B _ _ _ is meat that comes from a cow. E F E B

e Before babies can walk they c _ _ _ _ _ on hands and knees. W R A L C

f Mosquitoes can make you very ill with m _ _ _ _ _ _ _ . I L A R A M A

g When lots of animals run over dry earth they make a lot of d _ _ _ . S U T D

h Laura's legs a _ _ _ when she is ill. E C A H

2 Use the pictures to complete the puzzle.

GUESS WHAT

**What do you think happens in the next chapter?
Match the pictures and the sentences.**

a .... brings a big fat bird home for Christmas dinner.

b .... swims across the river on Christmas Day.

c .... brings the girls some Christmas presents.

d .... puts the presents in the girls' stockings.

e .... tells the girls about meeting Santa Claus.

f .... brings sweet potatoes for Christmas dinner.

g .... makes bread and cakes for Christmas dinner.

Chapter 7

Mr Edwards meets Santa Claus

The prairie had changed. Now the days were short and cold and the wind howled. Day after day the cold rain fell.

Mary and Laura played close to the fire and listened to the wet sound of rain. The nights were cold, but it never snowed. Every morning they saw only sad, wet grass. They wished they could see snow.

Laura was worried because **Christmas** was near, and **Santa Claus** could not travel without snow. Mary thought that, with or without snow, perhaps Santa Claus couldn't find them, so far away in **Indian Territory**.

'What day is it?' the girls asked Ma. 'How many more days until Christmas?' And they counted the days until there was only one more day to go.

Rain was still falling that morning. 'Perhaps there won't be a Christmas this year,' Laura said.

Still she went on hoping. But when Ma opened the door to let in some air and Laura heard the noise of the creek, she knew there was not going to be a Christmas that year. The creek was full and **roaring** with water. Santa Claus could not possibly cross it.

Pa came in, bringing a big fat **turkey**. 'How's that for a Christmas dinner?' he asked.

'Pa, is the water in the creek going down?' Mary asked.

'No, Mary, the water is moving fast. It'll be too dangerous for Mr Edwards to try to cross it now,' Pa replied.

Mr Edwards was invited to eat Christmas dinner with them, but now it looked impossible. 'No,' Pa said. 'I don't think Edwards will be here tomorrow.'

'Then Santa Claus can't come either,' said Mary.

Christmas
December 25, a holiday to remember the day when Jesus was born

Santa Claus this old man with red clothes and white hair is said to bring children presents at Christmas

Indian Territory land that belongs to Indians

roar to make a very loud, deep noise

turkey a bird that looks like a large chicken and is often eaten at Christmas

'It's too bad,' Ma said. 'But I know he hasn't forgotten you girls. He'll come next year, I'm sure.'

Still, Laura and Mary were not happy. It did not seem at all like Christmas. Even Pa did not want to play his fiddle.

After a long while, Ma suddenly stood up. 'I'm going to put up your **stockings**, girls,' she said. 'Perhaps something will happen.'

Laura's heart jumped. But then she remembered the roaring creek and felt sad. She and Mary watched Ma put their stockings over the fireplace. 'Now go to sleep,' Ma said, kissing them as they lay in their beds. 'Morning will come quicker if you're asleep.'

Then Laura heard Jack growl and someone crying, 'Ingalls! Ingalls!' When Pa opened the door, Laura saw that it was morning.

'Edwards! Come in, man! What's happened? Come sit by the fire!' Pa said.

Mr Edwards was shaking with cold. 'I swam across the creek,' he said. 'I carried my clothes on my head. But I'll be all right as soon as I get warm.'

'It was too dangerous, Edwards,' Pa said. 'We're happy you're here, but it was too dangerous for a Christmas dinner.'

'Your little ones needed a Christmas,' Mr Edwards replied. 'I had their presents from Independence, so no creek could stop me.'

Laura sat straight up in bed. 'Did you see Santa Claus in Independence?' she shouted.

'I sure did,' Mr Edwards said.

'Where? When? What did he look like? Did he really give you something for us?' Mary and Laura cried.

'Wait, wait a minute!' Mr Edwards laughed.

'I'll put Santa's presents in your stockings, girls,' said Ma, 'like Santa usually does. You mustn't look.'

They tried not to look at Ma as Mr Edwards answered all

stocking
something soft that you wear on your foot; children put up stockings at Christmas for Santa Claus to put presents in

43

their questions. When he saw the creek was so full, he said, he knew Santa Claus could not get across it.

'But *you* did,' said Laura.

'Yes, but I'm young. Santa Claus is too old and fat. I knew that Santa could only get as far south as Independence. So I walked to Independence and met Santa coming up the street, and the first thing he said to me was "Hello Edwards".'

'How did he know you?' asked Laura.

'Santa Claus knows everybody,' said Mr Edwards. 'And he said he knew two good little girls named Mary and Laura who lived by the Verdigris River. He asked me to bring your presents for him this year because with the water so high, he couldn't cross the creek himself. So here I am, sent by Santa Claus.'

Laura and Mary were silent a minute, thinking about that.

Then Ma said, 'You may look now, girls.'

Something was shining bright in the top of Laura's stocking. She jumped out of bed. So did Mary, but Laura beat her to the fireplace. And the shining thing was a bright new **tin** cup. Mary had one just like it.

These new tin cups were their very own. Now they each had a cup to drink from. Laura jumped up and down and shouted and laughed, but Mary stood still and looked with bright eyes at her own tin cup.

Then they reached into the stockings again. And they pulled out two long sticks of red and white **candy**. They looked and looked at that beautiful candy. Laura put her tongue on her candy, just to taste it, but Mary only looked at hers.

Those stockings were not empty yet. They each pulled out a little cake shaped like a heart. They had white sugar – like snow – on top and were too pretty to eat.

Laura and Mary just sat there, but then Ma said, 'Are you sure the stockings are empty?'

The girls put their arms down inside them again. And in the toe of each stocking was a shiny bright new **penny**! They

tin a cheap, soft, white metal

candy sweet food made of sugar or chocolate

penny a one-cent coin

could not speak. There had never been such a Christmas.

'Aren't you going to thank Mr Edwards?' Ma said gently.

'Oh, thank you, Mr Edwards! Thank you!' they said, and they meant it with all their hearts. Pa shook Mr Edwards' hand, and Pa and Ma and Mr Edwards looked like they were almost crying. Laura didn't know why.

Then Ma's eyes opened wide. Mr Edwards was taking **sweet potatoes** from his pockets. They were for Christmas dinner. Mr Edwards had brought them all the way from town, too.

'It's too much, Edwards,' Pa said. 'We can never thank you enough.'

For Christmas dinner there was the big, tasty turkey. There was bread that Ma had made, and there were the sweet potatoes. And after all that, they ate dried blackberries and little cakes.

Then Pa and Ma and Mr Edwards sat by the fire and talked about Christmas times back in Wisconsin. Mary and Laura looked at their beautiful cakes and played with their pennies. Little by little, they ate their sticks of candy. That was a happy Christmas.

sweet potato a vegetable that tastes sweet; it looks like a red potato and is yellow inside

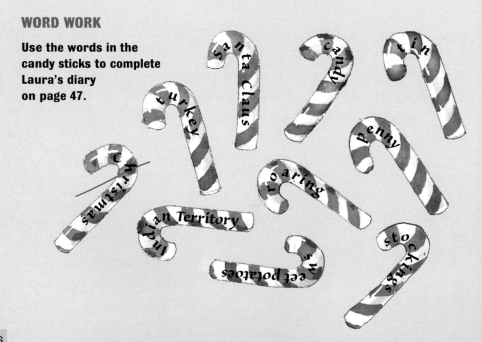

READING CHECK

Correct the mistakes in these sentences.

rains

a Christmas is near, and it ~~snows~~ a lot on the prairie.

b The creek is full of water, and Laura thinks that Santa Claus can cross it easily.

c Pa brings a big fat rabbit home for Christmas dinner.

d Mr Edwards is angry and shaking because he swam across the creek.

e Mr Edwards tells Laura and Carrie about meeting Santa Claus in Independence.

f The girls get tin plates, good things to eat and money for their Christmas presents.

g Mr Edwards doesn't stay for Christmas dinner with the family.

WORD WORK

Use the words in the candy sticks to complete Laura's diary on page 47.

Santa Claus

candy

tin

turkey

penny

Christmas

roaring

Indian Territory

sweet potatoes

stockings

At last – it's **(a)** Christmas ! Of course, we live in **(b)** .... and it isn't easy for **(c)** .... to visit us here. The river is very full and the water is **(d)** .... these days. We always eat **(e)** .... on Christmas Day and we sometimes eat **(f)** .... with it. We always put up our **(g)** .... the night before Christmas. This year Mary and I both got a **(h)** .... cup, a bright new **(i)** .... to put in our money boxes and some brightly coloured **(j)** .... to eat, too.

GUESS WHAT

What do you think happens in the next chapter? Tick the boxes.   **Yes**   **No**

a Pa eats and smokes together with an Indian chief.   ☐   ☐

b Two Indians come and take food and tobacco from the house.   ☐   ☐

c Jack bites one of the Indians on the leg.   ☐   ☐

d One of the Indians shoots Jack and kills him.   ☐   ☐

e Pa takes some animal skins to Independence to sell there.   ☐   ☐

f Pa brings a necklace from Independence for Ma.   ☐   ☐

Chapter 8

More and more Indians

The nights were still cold on the High Prairie, and the days were short and grey. Indians came riding on the path that passed so close to the house. They sat up straight on their naked horses and did not look right or left. But their black eyes shone. Mary and Laura sat against the house and looked up at them.

'I'm sorry I built the house so close to the Indian trail,' Pa said. 'But I thought they didn't use it any more.'

'Yes, there are so many Indians around here,' Ma said. 'I can't look up without seeing one.'

As she spoke she looked up, and there stood an Indian. He was in the doorway and they had not heard a sound.

'Oh, dear!' Ma whispered, frightened.

Jack jumped at the Indian. Pa caught him just in time.

'**How**!' the Indian said to Pa.

Pa held onto Jack and replied, 'How!' He pulled Jack over to the bed and tied him there. The Indian came in and sat down by the fire, and Pa sat down next to him. They sat there, friendly but not talking, while Ma finished cooking dinner.

Laura and Mary were quiet on their bed in the corner. They couldn't take their eyes from that Indian. He was so still that the beautiful **eagle** feathers in his hair did not move. He wore trousers made of animal skins, and his moccasins were covered with beads.

Pa and the Indian ate silently. Then Pa gave the Indian some tobacco for his pipe. They filled their pipes, lighted them, and silently smoked until the pipes were empty.

All this time nobody had said anything. But now the Indian said something to Pa. Pa shook his head and said, 'No

How an Indian word for hello

eagle a very large, strong bird

speak.' They all sat silent a while longer. Then the tall Indian got up and went away without a sound.

'Oh, dear!' Ma said again.

Pa said the Indian was an important man. 'He wore eagle feathers in his hair. I think he was an **Osage** Indian. I'm sure that was French he was speaking. I wish I spoke some French.'

'I think Indians should stay together with other Indians,' Ma said, 'and we'll do the same.'

'Don't worry, Caroline,' Pa said. 'That Indian was very friendly. And their camps down along the creek are quiet enough. If we're polite to them and watch Jack, we won't have any trouble.'

The very next morning when Pa opened the door, Laura saw Jack standing on the Indian trail, showing all his teeth. Right in front of him was the tall Indian, sitting very still on his horse. Jack looked ready to jump at them.

When the Indian saw Pa, he lifted his gun and pointed it straight at Jack. Pa ran to the trail and pulled Jack out of the way, and the Indian rode on.

'We were lucky that time!' Pa said. 'Well, it's his path. It was an Indian trail long before we came.'

After that, Jack was always tied up. He got crosser and crosser, but there was nothing Pa could do about it. 'If Jack hurts an Indian,' he said, 'there will be bad trouble.'

❋ ❋ ❋

Osage one kind of American Indian

Wild animals were wearing their thick winter **fur**, and Pa went hunting every day. He caught small animals and shot large ones for their fur. He carefully put the skins outside the house to dry in the sun. In the evenings he pulled the dry skins between his hands to make them soft, and every day the **bundle** of furs on the floor grew bigger. Laura loved to feel the soft fur in her fingers. Pa was saving all these furs to **trade** next spring in Independence.

One day when Pa was hunting, two Indians walked right into the house. They were dirty and cross. One of them looked at all the things in Ma's cupboard and took all the cornbread. The other took Pa's tobacco. Then one of them picked up the bundle of furs.

Ma held Baby Carrie in her arms, and Mary and Laura stood close to her. They looked at that Indian taking all Pa's furs but they couldn't do anything to stop him.

The Indian carried the furs as far as the door. Then the other Indian said something to him in an angry voice, and he dropped the bundle. They finally went away.

Ma sat down and pulled Mary and Laura close to her, and Laura felt Ma's heart beating.

'Well,' said Ma, smiling, 'I'm thankful they didn't take the **plough** and **seeds**.'

Laura was surprised. She asked, 'What plough?'

'Your Pa is going to trade that bundle of furs for a plough and lots of different seeds in the spring,' Ma said.

When Pa came home they told him about those Indians, and he looked serious. 'But all's well that ends well,' he said. 'And soon all the Indians here will move west.'

'Why do they go west?' Laura asked.

'When white settlers arrive in a place, the Indians have to move away from there.'

'But why?'

'The **government** makes them, Laura,' Pa said. 'That's

---

fur the hair on an animal's body

bundle a group of things that are kept or carried together

trade to give something that you have for something another person has

plough a large tool that is used on farms to cut up the ground in spring

seed when you put this in the ground a plant grows from it

government the people who control a country

why we're here. Lots of white people are going to come and live here. We came first to choose the best land. Now do you understand?'

'Yes, Pa,' Laura said. 'But, Pa, I thought this was Indian Territory. Won't the Indians be angry if they have to—'

'No more questions, Laura,' Pa said. 'It's time for bed.'

❈ ❈ ❈

Winter ended at last. The wind was softer, and the terrible cold was gone. One day Pa said it was time to take his furs to Independence.

Ma said, 'But the Indians are so near!'

'They're very friendly,' Pa said. 'I often meet them when I'm hunting in the forest. You needn't be afraid of them.'

'No,' Ma said. But Laura knew that Ma was afraid of Indians. 'You must go, Charles,' she said. 'We must have a plough and seeds. And you'll be back soon.'

The next morning before the sun came up, Pa got the horses ready, put the furs into the wagon, and drove away.

Laura and Mary counted the long, empty days. One, two, three, four, and still Pa had not come home. Ma said it was taking him a long time to trade his furs in town.

In the afternoon of the fifth day, Laura and Mary were playing a game outside. The weather was wild and sweet. The wind smelled like spring, and birds were flying north in the wide blue sky. Suddenly Mary stopped and said, 'What's that?'

Laura had already heard the strange noise. 'It's the Indians,' she said.

Mary stood still. She was frightened. Laura was not really afraid, but that noise made her feel strange. It was the sound of many Indian voices, something like an axe cutting wood or like a dog barking. It was wild, but it didn't seem angry.

Ma came outdoors and listened for a minute. Then she locked the animals in the stable. She told Laura and Mary to bring wood into the house. The sound was getting louder, now, and faster. It made Laura's heart beat fast.

'Come inside the house, now,' Ma said. She took Jack inside, too, and locked the door.

The sun went down and the sky turned bright pink. Ma was busy getting supper ready, but Laura and Mary watched from the window silently. All that time the sound from the creek got louder and louder, faster and faster. And Laura's heart beat faster and louder.

Then she heard Pa's wagon! Laura and Mary ran to the door and jumped on Pa, who had his arms full. Pa laughed his big laugh. 'What do you think I am,' he laughed, 'a tree to climb?' He dropped his bundles on the table and put his big arms around them.

'Listen to the Indians, Pa,' Laura said. 'Why are they making that strange noise?'

'Oh, they're having some kind of **jamboree**. I heard them when I crossed the creek.'

Then he went to put the horses and the new plough in the stable. When he came back, they opened the bundles. He had bought brown sugar, coffee, cornmeal, salt, and all the seeds that they needed. Then Pa gave Ma a packet. He watched her open it with his big smile. There was pretty cotton cloth in it for her to make herself a dress.

'Oh, Charles, you shouldn't! It's too much!' she cried. But her face shone with happiness.

Mary watched Pa quietly, but Laura climbed onto his leg and began beating him with her hands. 'Where is it? Where's my present?' she said, beating him.

Pa laughed his big laugh, like great bells ringing, and he pulled a packet out of his shirt pocket.

'You first, Mary,' he said, 'because you're waiting so quietly.' And he gave Mary a **comb** to wear in her hair. 'And here you are, Laura! This is for you,' he said.

The combs were just alike. They both had a bright star on

jamboree a big noisy party

comb a small piece of metal or plastic that you wear in your hair to keep it in place

the top. Mary's star was blue and Laura's was red. Ma put the combs in their hair. They laughed with excitement. They had never had anything so pretty.

Ma said, 'But Charles, you didn't get yourself a thing!'

'Oh, I got myself a plough,' said Pa. 'The weather will soon be warm enough to start using it.'

That was the happiest supper they had had in a long time. The salt pork that Pa had brought was very good. And Pa told them all about the seeds. He had got tobacco seeds and corn seeds, and the seeds of many different kinds of vegetables like carrots and potatoes.

'I tell you, Caroline, when these seeds grow in this rich land of ours, we'll be living like kings!' Pa said.

They had almost forgotten the wild noise from the Indian camps. But then Pa said something to Ma that made Laura sit very still and listen carefully.

'People in Independence say the government is going to move the white settlers out of Indian Territory.'

'Oh, no!' Ma said. 'Not when we have done so much.'

'Well, I don't believe what I heard,' Pa said. 'The government has always let settlers keep the land. I think they'll make the Indians move west again.'

Laura lay awake in bed a long time that night. She could still hear the noise of the wild jamboree in the Indian camp. Their fierce cries were carried on the screaming wind. They made her heart beat faster and faster and faster.

ACTIVITIES

READING CHECK

What do they say? Complete the sentences.

1 Come inside the house, now.

2 Where is it? Where's my present?

3 I'm sorry I built the house so close to the Indian trail.

4 No speak.

5 When white settlers arrive in a place the Indians have to move away.

6 I think Indians should stay together with other Indians.

a When Indians ride past the house Pa says *'I'm sorry I built the house so close to the Indian trail.'*

b .... says Pa to the Osage Indian.

c .... says Ma after the Osage Indian goes.

d .... says Pa to Laura.

e .... says Ma to Laura and Mary.

f .... says Laura to Pa.

WORD WORK

Find words in the square to complete the sentences on page 55.

```
K Y E F S A J B G
X B T L O D Y E O
F U R S E E D S V
B N A J A M B E E
S D D I C C A A R
P L E Y O P N G N
X E U P M P S L M
A J A M B O R E E
K W E T X V J R N
G P L O U G H V T
```

a The ...eagle... is a beautiful bird.

b Laura gets a .... for her hair.

c Pa wants to buy a ....

d Some people like wearing expensive .... coats.

e The .... decides what happens in a country.

f It's interesting to watch .... grow into plants.

g People .... things when they give one thing and get a different thing for it.

h A big Indian party is called a ....

i Pa has all his animal furs together in a ....

GUESS WHAT

Match the first and second parts of these sentences to find out what happens in the next chapter.

a Spring comes . . .

b Indians come . . .

c A fire comes very near . . .

d Mr Scott and Mr Edwards come . . .

1 to the house for food and tobacco.

2 to the prairie.

3 to talk to Pa about the Indians.

4 to the house but it isn't burnt.

Chapter 9 🌾

Prairie fire

Spring had come. The warm winds smelled exciting, and the outdoors was large and bright and sweet. Big white clouds were high up in the sky, and you could see their shadows over the prairie.

Pa was working hard, getting ready to plant potatoes. Pet and Patty were working hard, too, pulling the heavy plough. The plough was breaking up the grassy earth, and turning it over. Pa liked the land because it was so rich, and there wasn't a tree or stone in it.

Now many Indians came riding along the Indian trail. Indians were everywhere. Laura could hear their guns in the creeks when they were hunting. Indians often came to the house. Some of them were friendly, and some were not. All of them wanted food and tobacco, and Ma gave them what they wanted. But most of the food in the house was hidden.

Jack was miserable all the time. He was always tied up, and all the time he lay and hated the Indians. Laura and Mary were not surprised to see Indians any more. But they always felt safer near Pa or Jack.

One day they were helping Ma to get dinner ready. Baby Carrie was playing on the floor in the sun, and suddenly the light was gone.

'I think it's going to rain,' Ma said, looking out the window. Laura looked, too, and saw great black clouds in the south across the sun.

tub a big round open container made of wood where you can wash clothes

sack a large bag made of strong cloth

Pet and Patty came running from the field pulling the plough behind them and with Pa running after them.

'Prairie fire!' he shouted. 'Fill the **tub** with water! Put **sacks** in it! Hurry!'

Ma ran to the well, and Laura pulled the tub to it. Pa put the cows in the barn. Ma started pulling up water as fast as she could. Laura ran to get the sacks from the stable.

The sky was black now in the south, almost as dark as night. Pet and Patty were still pulling the plough, with Pa running behind them. Pa was making a long trench all the way around three sides of the house. He was shouting at the horses to make them hurry. Frightened rabbits came running across the prairie past Pa.

When the trench around the house was finished, Pa tied the horses to the house. The tub was full of water. Laura and Ma pushed the sacks into the water and made them very wet.

'Hurry, Caroline,' Pa shouted. 'The fire's coming faster than a horse can run.'

A big rabbit jumped right over the tub while Pa and Ma were lifting it. Ma told Laura to stay at the house. Pa and Ma carried the heavy tub all the way to the trench.

Laura stayed close to the house. She could see the red fire coming under the big black cloud of smoke. Jack was trembling and crying and staying close to Laura. The wind was blowing harder and screaming wildly. More and more rabbits came running. Birds screamed in the screaming wind. All the wild things on the prairie ran or jumped or flew as fast as they could go down to the creek.

Pa was going along the trench, making a small fire in the grass on the other side of it. Ma followed him with a wet sack, beating violently at the small fire when it crossed to her side of the trench. Soon Pa's small fire was burning along the other side of the trench all around the house. He and Ma fought it when it crossed the trench to their side. They beat it with the wet sacks, and did not let it come toward the house.

The big prairie fire was roaring now, roaring louder and louder in the screaming wind. Great **flames** turned and climbed high into the sky.

flame the bright light that you see when something is on fire

Mary and Laura stood against the house and held hands and trembled. Baby Carrie was in the house. Laura wanted to do something, but inside her head it was roaring like the fire. Her body shook. The smoke burned her nose, and her red eyes couldn't stop crying. Jack howled. The orange and yellow flames were coming faster than horses can run, and their terrible light danced over everything.

Pa's small fire burned slowly, moving away from the house. Slowly it went to meet the big wall of fire. And suddenly the big fire ate the little fire.

The wind screamed louder and the flames climbed all the way to the sky. Fire was all around the house.

Then suddenly it was all over. The fire roared past the house and was gone. Pa and Ma were beating little fires that burned here and there around the house. When those fires were out,

Ma came to the house to wash. Her skin was black with smoke, and she was trembling.

'Don't worry, girls,' she said. 'Pa's little fire saved us. And all's well that ends well.'

The air smelled of burned grass. Smoke was blowing in the wind. The wide prairie was black all the way to the line where the sky began. Everything felt different and miserable. But Pa and Ma were happy because the house was safe.

The animals came out of the creek. The birds came flying, the rabbits jumped slowly and looked, and the prairie chickens came out walking.

❄ ❄ ❄

That night Mr Edwards and Mr Scott came to see Pa. They were worried.

'Maybe the Indians started the fire to frighten us. Maybe they want all the white settlers to leave,' Mr Scott said.

'I don't believe it,' said Pa. 'The Indians have always burned the prairie to make the green grass grow more quickly. And it's easier for them to ride their horses in shorter grass.'

While they were talking, they could hear the **drums** that were beating in the camps, and the shouts of the Indians.

Laura sat quietly listening to the talk and to the Indians.

'There are too many Indians in those camps,' said Mr Edwards. 'I don't like it.'

'The only good Indian is a dead Indian,' Mr Scott said.

'I don't know,' Pa said. 'I think the Indians are as good as anyone, if they are left alone. But the government has moved them west so many times. Naturally, they hate white settlers, but they're afraid of the white soldiers at **Fort** Dodge and Fort Gibson. I don't think they'll make any trouble.'

'Why are so many of them in the camps?' asked Mr Scott.

'They're just getting ready to hunt **buffalo**,' Pa said.

'Well,' Mr Scott said slowly, 'I hope you're right, Ingalls. I really hope you're right.'

drum you play music on this by hitting it with your hand or a stick

fort a strong building where soldiers live

buffalo a large animal like a cow with a very large head and thick hair

READING CHECK

Circle the best words to complete these sentences.

a Pa is getting ready to plant (potatoes) apple trees   flowers .

b None   Not all   All   of the Indians who come to the house are friendly.

c Jack doesn't attack the Indians because   he's tied up   he likes them now   he's lazy .

d Pa makes a   trench   trail   path   all round the house.

e Pa makes a small   river   fire   wall   and Ma stops it from getting bigger with a wet sack.

f Pa's fire   stops the big fire from burning   helps the big fire to burn   burns   the house.

g Mr Scott thinks that the Indians started the fire to   frighten white settlers   make the grass shorter   get ready for the buffalo hunt .

h Mr Scott   Pa   Mr Edwards   thinks the Indians won't make any more trouble.

i The Indians are afraid of   white soldiers   white settlers   fire .

WORD WORK

Find words in the fire to match the pictures on page 61.

a .....roar.........

b ....

c ....

d ....

e ....

f ....

GUESS WHAT

What do you think happens in the last chapter? Tick two boxes.

a ☐ Indians attack the house.

b ☐ Different Indian tribes argue together.

c ☐ All the Indians leave and go west.

d ☐ Soldiers come to live in the Little House.

e ☐ Indians burn the Little House to the ground.

f ☐ Laura and her family leave the Little House.

Chapter 10

Indian war-cry

The next day Pa worked in the field, getting it ready to plant the seeds. He came in at noon, black from the burned prairie, but he was pleased. He didn't have to worry about the tall grass any more.

But he began to worry about the Indians. More and more of them were camping near the creek. Mary and Laura saw the smoke from their fires by day, and at night they heard fierce shouts.

When shadows began to fall on the prairie and the wind was quiet, the noises from the Indian camps grew louder and wilder. Pa shut the horses and cows in the stable and brought Jack into the house. No one could go outdoors until morning. In her sleep Laura heard the wild noises and beating drums.

One night Pa sat by the fireplace making **bullets**. Laura and Mary lay awake and watched him.

'Why are you doing that, Pa?' Mary asked.

'Oh, I have nothing better to do,' Pa said. But Laura knew he was tired from working in the field and wanted to sleep.

No more Indians came to the house. Mary did not want to go out of the house any more, so Laura had to play outside by herself. But she felt strange there. The prairie didn't feel safe any more.

Mr Scott and Mr Edwards, with their guns, came and talked to Pa in the field one day. At dinner, Pa told Ma that some of the settlers were talking about building a **stockade**. 'I told Scott and Edwards that it wasn't a good idea. If we need one, we'll need it before we can build it. And the worst thing is to show that we're afraid.'

Laura wondered why Pa was talking this way. Pa was never

bullet a small piece of metal that you use in a gun

stockade high walls made of wood around a place; they are built to keep people safe inside

afraid. But she was. Every night the Indian drums beat faster and faster, and their cries got wilder and wilder.

In the middle of the night, Laura sat straight up in bed and screamed. A terrible sound had woken her. Ma came quickly and said in her gentle way, 'Be quiet, Laura. You mustn't frighten Carrie.'

The house was dark, but Ma was still wearing her dress. She had not gone to bed. Pa stood by the window, looking out. He had his gun. Then that terrible sound came again.

'What is it?' Laura screamed. 'What is it? Oh, Pa, what is it?'

Pa said, 'It's the Indian **war-cry**, Laura.'

Ma made a soft sound, and he said to her, 'They need to know, Caroline.'

He explained that the Indians were dancing around their fires and talking about war. 'But I'm here and Jack's here,' Pa said, 'and there are soldiers at Fort Dodge. So don't be afraid, Mary and Laura.'

'No, Pa,' Laura said. But she was terribly afraid. The drums seemed to beat inside her head. The wild howls were worse than wolves.

Then they heard the sound of a running horse. It came nearer and nearer. In the light of the moon, Laura saw a little black horse with an Indian on its back. The Indian had a blanket around him, feathers on his head, and a gun at his side. He rode by as fast as the wind, and then he was gone.

'That was the tall Osage Indian who came to the house once and talked French to me!' Pa said. 'What's he doing out at this hour, riding so fast?'

Nobody answered because nobody knew.

The next day they could not go out of the house. There was not one sound from the Indian camps. The whole wide prairie was still. But that night the noise in the camps was worse than the night before. The war-cries were terrible. Pa

war-cry a shout used by people to frighten their enemy

63

quarrel to argue angrily with someone

watched at the window with his gun, Laura and Mary stayed close to Ma, and poor little Carrie cried. Jack growled all night long, and he howled when the war-cries came.

Night after night, the Indians shouted and danced and beat their drums. All up and down the creek, war-cries answered war-cries. The sound filled the prairie. There was no rest. Laura ached all over.

The silent days were worse than the nights. The animals stayed in the stable. Mary and Laura could not go out of the house. And Pa watched and listened all the time. He didn't eat much. One day his head fell onto the table and he slept a little. He was so tired. But in a minute he woke up with a jump and said, crossly, to Ma, 'Don't let me do that again!'

That night was the worst night of all. The drums beat faster and the war cries made their blood run cold.

At the window Pa said, 'Caroline, they're **quarrelling** among themselves. Maybe they'll fight each other.'

'Oh, Charles, I hope so!' Ma said.

All night long there was not a minute's rest. Just before the sun came up, the last war-cry ended and Laura fell asleep in Ma's arms.

She woke up in bed. The door was open, and the sun was high in the sky. It was already noon. Ma was cooking dinner and Pa was sitting outside on the step.

He said to Ma, 'There's another big group, going off to the south.'

Laura went to the door and saw a long line of Indians far away. Pa told her that two long lines of Indians had gone west that morning. Now this one was going south. It meant that the Indians had argued among themselves and were not going to hunt buffalo together.

'Tonight we'll sleep!' Pa said, and they did. They did not even dream. In the morning Pa took his gun and went down the creek road. Laura and Mary and Ma stayed in the house and waited the whole long day.

When Pa came back in the late afternoon, he said everything was all right. He had gone up and down the creek and seen many empty Indian camps. All the Indian **tribes** had left, except the Osages.

He had met an Osage in the forest who could speak English. He told Pa that all the tribes except the Osages wanted to kill the settlers. The tall Indian had ridden so far and so fast that night because he did not want them to kill the white people. He was an Osage **chief**, and his name was Great Soldier.

'He went on arguing with them day and night,' Pa said, 'until the other Osages agreed with him. Then he told the other tribes that the Osages were ready to fight them to save the white settlers.'

That was why there had been so much noise in the camps. The Indian tribes were howling at each other. In the end, the other tribes did not want to fight Great Soldier and the Osages. So they went away.

'That's one good Indian!' Pa said.

※ ※ ※

There was another long night of sleep. In the morning Pa opened the door to let in the warm spring air. He stood on the step, looking east, and he said, 'Come here, Caroline. And you, Mary and Laura.'

Laura ran out first, and she was surprised. The Indians were coming. First came the tall Indian chief who had saved

tribe a group of Indians

chief the most important person in a tribe of Indians

basket a container that is usually made of thin pieces of wood

their lives. His black horse was very near now, and Laura's heart beat fast. She looked at the Indian's moccasins, at his colourful blanket, at his naked brown-red arms that carried the long gun. His face was still and fierce. Only the long eagle feathers in his hair moved in the wind.

'Great Soldier himself,' Pa said softly. He lifted his hand to say hello.

But the horse and the Indian chief went by without looking at Pa or Ma or Mary or Laura or the house. Then other horses and Indians with eagle feathers in their hair went by. Brown face after brown face went by. Bright beads shone in the sun, and horses' tails and eagle feathers blew in the wind.

The women and children came riding behind the Indian men. Little naked brown Indians, no bigger than Mary and Laura, went riding by. They did not have to wear clothes. All their skin was out in the air. Their straight black hair blew in the wind and their black eyes shone with happiness.

Laura looked and looked at the Indian children, and they looked at her. She had a sudden wish to be a little Indian girl, to ride naked in the wind and the sun.

Then Indian mothers came riding by with babies in **baskets** at the sides of their horses. Laura looked straight into the bright eyes of one little baby. Its eyes were black as a night when no stars shine.

'Pa,' she said, 'get me that little Indian baby!'

'Be quiet, Laura!' Pa said.

The baby's head turned and its eyes looked into Laura's eyes.

'Oh, I want it! I want it!' Laura cried. 'It wants to stay with me. Please, Pa, please!'

'Quiet, Laura,' Pa said. 'The Indian woman wants to keep her baby.'

Then Laura began to cry. The little papoose was gone. She was never going to see it again.

'I've never heard of such a thing,' Ma said. 'Why do you want an Indian baby, of all things?'

'Its eyes are so black,' Laura cried. She could not say what she meant.

No one was hungry for dinner. Pa and Ma and Mary and Laura stayed by the door and looked at the long line of Indians until nothing was left but silence and emptiness. All the world seemed very quiet and lonely.

❋ ❋ ❋

One morning the whole prairie was green. Pa hurried into the field with the horses and his plough, and Mary and Laura helped Ma plant the seeds for the vegetables. They were all so happy because spring had come.

'Soon we'll have vegetables to eat and we'll live like kings!' Pa said.

One day Mary and Laura were washing dishes in the house when they heard Pa's voice, loud and angry. They looked out and saw Mr Edwards and Mr Scott in the field with Pa.

'No, Scott!' said Pa. 'I won't stay here until the soldiers take me away like a criminal. The government in Washington told us it was all right to build our houses here. But if now they want us to go, we'll go. We won't wait for the soldiers to make us leave. We're going now!'

'What's the matter, Charles? Where are we going?' Ma asked.

'I don't know, Caroline! But we're going. We're leaving here,' Pa said. 'Scott and Edwards say the government is sending soldiers to make the settlers leave Indian Territory.'

His face was very red and his eyes were like blue fire. Laura was frightened; she had never seen Pa look like that.

'I'm going, too,' said Mr Edwards.

'Take the cow and the calf,' Pa said to Mr Scott. 'You've been a good neighbour, and I'm sorry to leave you. But we're going in the morning.'

After Mr Scott left with the animals, Mr Edwards and Pa shook hands and said goodbye. Then he shook hands with Ma and said, 'Goodbye, Mrs Ingalls. I'll never forget how kind you were to me.'

Mary said politely, 'Goodbye, Mr Edwards.' But Laura forgot to be polite. She said, 'Oh, Mr Edwards, please don't go away! Oh, Mr Edwards, thank you, thank you for going all the way to Independence to find Santa Claus for us.'

Mr Edwards eyes shone very bright, and he went away without saying another word.

Pa began to put the canvas cover on the wagon and Laura and Mary knew it was true; they really were going away.

Everyone was quiet that night. Ma looked sad and said

gently, 'A year gone, Charles.' But Pa answered with a smile, 'What's a year? We have all the time in the world.'

The next morning, Pa and Ma packed the wagon. First Ma laid two beds across the back of the wagon. Then she and Pa packed the clothes, the food, and the dishes. The only thing they could not take was the plough.

Laura and Mary climbed into the wagon and sat on the bed in the back. Ma put Baby Carrie between them. Ma climbed to her place on the seat. Then suddenly Laura wanted to see the house again. So Pa opened the back of the wagon cover, and Mary and Laura looked out at their little log house.

Pa climbed to his place beside Ma and took the reins in his hands. Jack went under the wagon, and Pet and Patty walked away from the little house on the prairie.

As far as they could see, to the east and to the south and to the west, nothing was moving. Only the green grass was waving in the wind.

'It's a great country, Caroline,' Pa said. 'But there will be wild Indians and wolves here for many years.'

Pa and Ma were still and silent, and Mary and Laura were quiet, too. But Laura felt all excited inside. You never know what will happen next, nor where you will be tomorrow, when you are travelling in a covered wagon.

READING CHECK

Are these sentences true or false? Tick the boxes.

		True	False
a	More and more Indians camp near the creek.	✔	☐
b	The Indian camps are very noisy during the day.	☐	☐
c	Pa, Mr Edwards, and Mr Scott get ready to fight.	☐	☐
d	Pa talks about himself, Jack, and the soldiers at Fort Dodge to make Laura less afraid.	☐	☐
e	The Indian tribes all go to hunt buffalo together.	☐	☐
f	The Osages were ready to fight other Indians to save the settlers.	☐	☐
g	Pa gets Laura a little Indian baby.	☐	☐
h	Pa gives the cow and calf to Mr Scott.	☐	☐
i	The Ingalls family leave their house when soldiers tell them to go.	☐	☐
j	Mr Edwards leaves, too.	☐	☐
k	Pa can't take the plough with him.	☐	☐
l	Mary and Laura look out at the house from the back of the wagon when they leave.	☐	☐

WORD WORK

Match the words in the blanket with the definitions on page 71.

a ...*bullet*... a piece of metal that you use in a gun

b .... high walls around a place

c .... a shout before fighting

d .... to argue angrily

e .... a group of Indians

f .... an important person in a group of Indians

g .... a container

GUESS WHAT

What happens to the little house on the prairie after the Ingalls family moves out? Choose from these ideas.

a ☐ An Indian family moves into it.

b ☐ Another settler family moves into it.

c ☐ It stays empty and after some time it falls down.

d ☐ It stays empty but travellers use it to stay in at night on long journeys.

e ☐ A businessman makes it bigger and opens it as a small hotel for travellers.

Project A   *Memories*

1 Read these memories and match them with the pictures on page 73.

1 The most exciting holiday I've ever had was in New Zealand, there were so many things to do – swimming with dolphins, visiting hot springs, skiing. It was great.

The nicest Christmas I've ever had was a couple of years ago at my cousins' house. I liked it because all the family was there and we sang Christmas Carols and I had lots of sweets. TJ

2 The scariest thing I remember was when I went sailing last summer with my sister. W were in the middle of a lake, but we didn't know how to sail. Every time we turned, we thought the boat was going to go under the water.

The most annoying thing happened to me a few weeks ago. We had a cross-country ra at school and there was a cup for the winner Usually I'm the fastest girl in the school. But that day another girl won and I came second was really annoyed.

My funniest memory is my dad's fiftieth birthday party. He started dancing and suddenly he slipped in some water on the flo from the dog's bowl, and he landed on his ba We all laughed a lot – my dad, too!   Amy

3 The best song I've ever heard is '8 Mile' by Eminem. I really like the way that he raps.

The most shocking thing that I remember was when we had a big fire one night in our barbecue. Luckily my dad put it out quickly and no one was hurt.   Ben

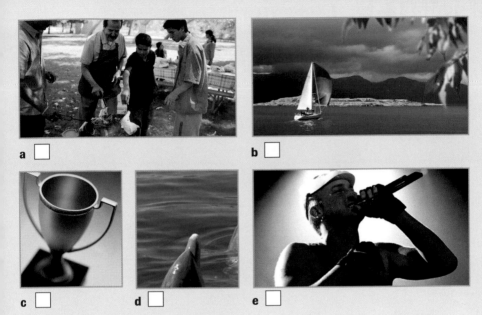

a ☐   b ☐

c ☐   d ☐   e ☐

2 **Write about your memories.**
   Use these words.

the scariest

the most exciting

the best

the most shocking

the most annoying

the nicest

the funniest

Project B · *Describing a picture*

1 Look at the picture and complete the description.

This picture shows a Wild West settler landscape from *Little House on the Prairie*. In the background on the left we can just see the **(a)**........................ through the dark green trees. On the right we can see the **(b)**..................... with the horses, **(c)**........................ and **(d)**.................. standing in front of it. Pa is holding the **(e)**........................ In the background on the right, we can just see some Indians on the Indian **(f)**........................ . More or less in the middle of the picture we can see the Ingalls family's lovely little **(g)**..................... house with its front window, its wooden **(h)**....................... on top, and its **(i)**........................ made from mud and rocks. **(j)**........................ is standing at the door with **(k)**........................ in her arms. In the foreground, **(l)**........................ and **(m)**........................ are playing with **(n)**........................ the dog.

PROJECTS

2 Look at the beads. They show adjective order.

FEELING · SIZE · SHAPE · AGE · COLOUR · STYLE · MATERIAL

For example

a pretty, little, old, multicoloured bead necklace

Put these descriptions in order. Use the beads above and a dictionary to help you.

a

stone big fireplace white

a ....

d

smelly skunk black and white skins new

....

b

statue pretty china pink

a ....

e

big lovely wooden table round

a ....

c

nice curtains cotton checked red and white

....

f

multicoloured quilt patchwork beautiful

a ....

3 Look at the picture. Complete the notes below.

This picture shows the inside of Wild West settlers' . . .
In the background, we can just see . . .

In the middle of the picture . . .

In the foreground . . .

4 Write a description from your notes.

GRAMMAR CHECK

Wish

We use wish + Past Simple to talk about things that we would like to be true in the present, but which aren't.

I wish I spoke some French. (= but I don't)

Note that can changes to could.

I wish Jack could ride with us. (= but he can't)

Note that will changes to would.

I wish she would stop crying. (= but she won't)

1 Write the second sentences to complete Laura's words.

a The house smells terrible now. I / wish / Indians / not wear / skunk skins

.... *I wish Indians didn't wear skunk skins.* ....

b They often come and take things from our house.

Ma / wish / they / will not take / our things

....

c Indians sometime try to speak to Pa. he / wish / he / can / speak / the Indian language

....

d Ma doesn't feel safe because Pa is away. she / wish / he / be / at home

....

e We have to tie up Jack to stop him from biting an Indian.

Jack / wish / he / can run and play

....

f We live very close to an Indian trail.

Pa / wish / the house / not be / so close to the trail

....

g My baby sister can't wear necklaces.

I / wish / I / have / her necklace

....

h The mosquitoes are terrible in the summer.

we / wish / they / will not bite / us

....

Gerund with sense verbs

The gerund (–ing form) is the noun form of a verb. To make the gerund, we usually add –ing to the verb, but when a verb ends in a consonant + –e, we remove the –e and add –ing. When a verb ends in a short vowel + consonant, we double the consonant and add –ing.

talk – talking   ride – riding   sit – sitting

We use the gerund after sense verbs such as see, watch, hear, imagine, and feel.

They watched snakes lying still in the sun.

She could see the red fire coming under the big black cloud of smoke.

2 Complete the letter. Use the *–ing* form of the verbs in brackets.

Dear Grandma and Grandpa,

I can imagine you a) ...reading... (read) this letter. We're living in a beautiful house on a prairie. There are lots of animals! We often see rabbits b) .... (run) through the long grass, and this morning I found a snake c) .... (lie) outside our front door. There are wolves here, too. One night, we heard them d) .... (howl) outside the house. We were very frightened. Now Pa has built a strong door and we feel safe, but sometimes I think of them e) .... (walk) around outside.

We're near to an Indian camp, too. Pa often sees Indians f) .... (hunt) when he goes into the forest, and sometimes we hear them g) .... (dance) around their camp fires at night. We're very happy here, but it's going to be very cold in the winter. Yesterday we watched some birds h) .... (fly) south. They can feel the cold weather i) .... (come), and they are leaving.

I have to finish this letter now so Pa can take it into Independence. And I can hear baby Carrie j) .... (cry). Perhaps she can smell Ma k) .... (cook) a prairie chicken, and she's hungry!

From your loving granddaughter, Mary

GRAMMAR CHECK

Modal auxiliary verbs: may, might, could, ought to, and should

We use may (not) + infinitive without *to*, might (not) + infinitive without *to*, and could (not) + infinitive without *to* to talk about actions and events that are (or are not) possible.

Jack might bite an Indian.

A log was falling towards Ma. Pa couldn't stop it.

We use ought + infinitive or should + infinitive without *to* to give advice about what is the right thing to do.

I ought to make a strong door.

We should have thick walls around us.

We use shouldn't + infinitive without *to* to form negative statements.

You shouldn't play far from the house. (= it's a bad thing to do)

3 **Choose the correct word or words to complete the conversation.**

Scott: The Indians a) **could**/couldn't attack us at any time. I think we b) **should/may** build a stockade. What do you think, Ingalls?

Pa: Yes, the Indians c) **should/could** attack us, but I don't think they will – and we d) **may not/shouldn't** show them we're afraid.

Edwards: I agree with Ingalls. Anyway, they e) **might/ought to** see us building a stockade and decide to attack us before we can finish it.

Scott: Well, I don't like it. They're preparing for a war, and we f) **couldn't/ought to** prepare, too.

Pa: They g) **might/should** be preparing for a war, but we don't know that – they h) **couldn't/could** just be here to hunt buffalo.

Scott: Yes, but we i) **shouldn't/may** do nothing and hope the Indians are here to hunt buffalo. That would be crazy. We j) **shouldn't/should** protect our families.

Pa: You k) **could/might not** take your family and go into Independence. It's your choice, Scott, but I'm staying here.

GRAMMAR CHECK

Too and enough/not enough

We use too + adjective to say that something is more than necessary. We can add to + infinitive after the adjective to give more information about what we can or can't do as a result.

They gave me the calf because it was too small to travel.

We use adjective + enough to say that something is as much as necessary. We can add to + infinitive after *enough* to give more information about what we can or can't do as a result.

It wasn't a big wagon, but it was big enough to carry everything.

We use not + adjective + enough to say that something is not as much as necessary.

Pa was sick, so he was not strong enough to help the girls.

4 Write the sentences with *too*, *enough* or *not enough*.

a The day after the wolves came, the children were very scared.

they / not be / brave / play / outside

They weren't brave enough to play outside.

b Carrie didn't know who the Indians were. she / not be / old / understand

....

....

c The cowboys gave Pa a cow. it / be / thin / sell

....

....

d Santa Claus didn't come. the river / be / dangerous / cross

....

....

e One day Pa saw a deer. he / not be / quick / shoot it

....

....

f Pa had to cut the prairie grass. it / be / tall / plant new seeds in it

....

g Pa was pleased after the fire. the grass / be / short / use / the plough

....

GRAMMAR CHECK

Past Simple + Past Simple and Past Simple + Past Continuous

We use Past Simple + and + Past Simple to talk about two past actions that happened close in time or one after the other.

We went outside and started to play.

We use Past Simple + while + Past Simple when two past actions happened at the same time and were equally long.

He sang while he worked.

We use the Past Simple + Past Continuous when a shorter past action happens in the middle of a longer past action. We use the time expressions while and when to show the relationship between the two past actions. We use while in front of the Past Continuous verb and when in front of the Past Simple verb.

She was talking to Jack when he suddenly growled.

Jack suddenly growled while she was talking to him.

5 Match the sentence halves.

a Laura held the door
b Pa saw fifty wolves
c While they were all sleeping,
d The wolves walked around the house and
e Laura was sitting up in bed

f Pa held his gun while he
g They couldn't sleep
h The next day Pa got up early

1 tried to smell the people inside.
2 while Pa put the hinges on it.
3 while he was riding home.
4 while the wolves were walking around outside.
5 was standing by the window, watching the wolves.
6 the wolves came to the house.
7 while the girls were still sleeping.
8 when a wolf suddenly howled on the other side of the wall.

GRAMMAR CHECK

So

We can use *so* to talk about the reasons why we do things.

The other tribes didn't want to fight the Great Soldier, so they went away.

We can also use *so* + adjectives to mean *really* or *very*.

'I'm sorry I built the house so close to the Indian trail.'

'Patty was trembling all over,' Pa said. 'She was so scared.'

6 **Complete the sentences with what *so* + the adjectives in the box.**

big	fast	~~high~~	beautiful	deep	frightened

a The flames were ..*so high*.., they reached up to the sky.

b 'Why is that Indian riding .... at this time of night, Charles?' asked Ma.

c Pa had to swim across the river because it was ....

d The beads were .... , Laura wanted to keep them.

e Patty wanted to run because she was .... of the wolves.

f The wolves were .... , they were bigger than Laura.

7 **Match the sentence halves.**

a The house didn't have a roof,

b Some of the settlers were scared,

c It was difficult to move the cattle across the river,

d Ma and Pa wanted the Indians to be friendly,

e Pa was worried about the wolves,

f Pa couldn't finish the house alone,

1 so the cowboys asked Pa to help them.

2 so he built a stable for the horses.

3 so they wanted to build a stockade.

4 so Mr Edwards helped him.

5 so Pa put the canvas wagon cover over it to keep the rain out.

6 so they gave them food and tobacco.

GRAMMAR CHECK

Comparative adjectives: repeating for emphasis

To make comparative adjectives, we add –er to most short adjectives.	*cold – colder*
When adjectives finish in –e, we add –r.	*late – later*
When adjectives finish in a consonant + y, we change the y to i and add –er.	*happy – happier*
When adjectives finish in a short vowel + consonant, we double the consonant and add –er.	*big – bigger*
With longer adjectives, we put more before the adjective.	*comfortable – more comfortable*

We can use comparative adjective + and + repeated comparative adjective when we want to emphasize something.

The Indians came closer and closer.

With longer adjectives, we use more and more + adjective.

Life became more and more difficult for the settlers.

8 **Complete the text. Use the comparative form of the adjectives in brackets + *and* + the repeated comparative.**

Pa drove the wagon, and Laura and Mary looked back at the house. It got a) ..smaller and smaller.. (small). Laura wanted to cry, but she knew that she had to be brave.

Every day, the Rocky Mountains to the west of them started to look b) .... (big). The summer was coming, and the weather was getting c) .... (warm). There were flowers everywhere, and the mountain rivers were full of water. They became d) .... (difficult) to cross. Laura missed their house on the prairie, but she felt e) .... (good) every day.

One day they saw a big group of Indians on horses. They were coming f) .... (close) across the prairie. Pa's face became g) .... (worried). 'Get back into the wagon, girls!' he said.

Dominoes is an enjoyable series of illustrated classic and modern stories in four carefully graded language stages – from Starter to Three – which take learners from beginner to intermediate level.

Each *Domino* reader includes:

- a good story to read and enjoy
- integrated activities to develop reading skills and increase active vocabulary
- personalized projects to make the language and story themes more meaningful
- seven pages of grammar activities for consolidation.

Each *Domino* pack contains a reader, plus a MultiROM with:

- a complete audio recording of the story, fully dramatized to bring it to life
- interactive activities to offer further practice in reading and language skills and to consolidate learning.

If you liked this Level Three *Domino*, why not read these?

The Last of the Mohicans
James Fenimore Cooper

The year is 1757. The English and the French are at war in North America. Two sisters – Cora and Alice – want to visit their father, General Munro. They begin their dangerous journey with the handsome English officer, Duncan Heyward and the Indian guide, Magua. On the way they meet friends and enemies, and many adventures. Some people will become heroes and some people will die. But what will happen to their friend Uncas, the last of the Mohican Indians?

Book ISBN: 978 0 19 424818 1
MultiROM Pack ISBN: 978 0 19 424776 4

Revolution
Jann Huizenga and Linda Huizenga

'All men are created equal . . .'

When Thomas Jefferson wrote these words in June 1776, in the American Declaration of Independence, he started something that was very much bigger than he imagined.

This book looks at the history around that Declaration, and at the Revolution that led to the birth of the United States of America.

Book ISBN: 978 0 19 424826 6
MultiROM Pack ISBN: 978 0 19 424784 9

You can find details and a full list of books in the *Dominoes* catalogue and Oxford English Language Teaching Catalogue, and on the website: www.oup.com/elt

Teachers: see www.oup.com/elt for a full range of online support, or consult your local office.

	CEFR	Cambridge Exams	IELTS	TOEFL iBT	TOEIC
Level 3	B1	PET	4.0	57-86	550
Level 2	A2–B1	KET-PET	3.0-4.0	–	–
Level 1	A1–A2	YLE Flyers/KET	3.0	–	–
Starter & Quick Starter	A1	YLE Movers	–	–	–